Interactive SCIENCE™

Go to PearsonTexas.com to learn science through videos, labs, online activities, and more!

PEARSON Texas.com

Glenview, Illinois • Boston, Massachusetts • Chandler, Arizona • Hoboken, New Jersey

PEARSON

Texas Science • Texas Science • Texas Science • Texas Science • Texas Science • Texas Science • Texas Science

You are an author!

You are one of the authors of this book. You can write in this book! You can take notes in this book! You can draw in it too! This book will be yours to keep.

Print your name, school, and city or town below. Then write to tell everyone all about you.

My Photo

Name

School

City or Town

All About Me

Acknowledgments appear on pages EM31–EM32, which constitute an extension of this copyright page.

Copyright © 2015 Pearson Education, Inc., or its affiliates. All Rights Reserved. Printed in the United States of America. This publication is protected by copyright, and permission should be obtained from the publisher prior to any prohibited reproduction, storage in a retrieval system, or transmission in any form or by any means, electronic, mechanical, photocopying, recording, or likewise. For information regarding permissions, write to Rights Management & Contracts, Pearson Education, Inc., 221 River Street, Hoboken, New Jersey 07030.

Pearson, Scott Foresman, Pearson Scott Foresman, Lab Zone, Pearson Flipped Videos for Science, and Planet Diary are trademarks, in the U.S. and/or other countries, of Pearson Education, Inc., or its affiliates.

Untamed Science is a US registered mark licensed to Pearson from EcoMedia.

PEARSON

Softcover: ISBN-13: 978-0-328-80748-2
ISBN-10: 0-328-80748-6
10 19

Hardcover: ISBN-13: 978-0-328-80327-9
ISBN-10: 0-328-80327-8
4 5 6 7 8 9 10 V011 18 17 16 15 14

ON THE COVER
Pygmy owls can hunt prey larger than themselves.

Program Authors

DON BUCKLEY, M.Sc.

Director of Technology & Innovation,
The School at Columbia University, New York, New York
Don Buckley has transformed learning spaces, textbooks, and media resources so that they work for students and teachers. He has advanced degrees from leading European universities, is a former industrial chemist, published photographer, and former consultant to MOMA's Education Department. He also teaches a graduate course at Columbia Teacher's College in Educational Technology and directs the Technology and Innovation program at the school. He is passionate about travel, architecture, design, change, the future, and innovation.

ZIPPORAH MILLER, M.A.Ed.

Associate Executive Director for Professional Development Programs and Conferences, National Science Teachers Association, Arlington, Virginia
Mrs. Miller is currently the associate executive director for professional development programs and conferences at NSTA. She provides professional development and e-learning opportunities to science educators nationwide. She is a former K–12 science supervisor and STEM coordinator for the Prince George's County Public School District in Maryland. During her tenure there, she served as teacher, STEM coordinator, principal, and administrator. Mrs. Miller is passionate about providing quality educational opportunities to all students.

MICHAEL J. PADILLA, Ph.D.

Eugene P. Moore School of Education, Clemson University, Clemson, South Carolina
A former middle school teacher and a leader in middle school science education, Dr. Michael Padilla has served as president of the National Science Teachers Association and as a writer of the 1996 National Science Education Standards. He is a professor of science education at Clemson University. As lead author of the *Science Explorer* series, Dr. Padilla has inspired the team in developing a program that promotes student inquiry and meets the needs of today's students.

KATHRYN THORNTON, Ph.D.

Professor, Mechanical & Aerospace Engineering,
University of Virginia,
Charlottesville, Virginia
Selected by NASA in May 1984, Dr. Kathryn Thornton is a veteran of four space flights. She has logged more than 975 hours in space, including more than 21 hours of extravehicular activity. As an author on the *Scott Foresman Science* series, Dr. Thornton's enthusiasm for science has inspired teachers around the globe.

MICHAEL E. WYSESSION, Ph.D.

Associate Professor of Earth and Planetary Science,
Washington University, St. Louis, Missouri
An author on more than 50 scientific publications, Dr. Wysession was awarded the prestigious Packard Foundation Fellowship and Presidential Faculty Fellowship for his research in geophysics. Dr. Wysession is an expert on Earth's inner structure and has mapped various regions of Earth using seismic tomography. He is known internationally for his work in geoscience education and research, and was an author of the Next Generation Science Standards.

Planet Diary Author

JACK HANKIN

Science/Mathematics Teacher,
The Hilldale School, Daly City, California
Founder, Planet Diary Web site
Mr. Hankin is the creator and writer of Planet Diary, a science current events Web site. Mr. Hankin is passionate about bringing science news and environmental awareness into classrooms.

Activities Author

KAREN L. OSTLUND, Ph.D.

President-Elect, National Science Teachers Association, Arlington, Virginia
Dr. Ostlund has over 40 years of experience teaching at the elementary, middle school, and university levels. She was Director of WINGS Online (Welcoming Interns and Novices with Guidance and Support) and the Director of the UTeach/Dell Center for New Teacher Success with the UTeach program in the College of Natural Sciences at the University of Texas at Austin. She also served as Director of the Center for Science Education at the University of Texas at Arlington, as President of the Council of Elementary Science International, and as a member of the Board of Directors of the National Science Teachers Association. As an author of Scott Foresman Science, Dr. Ostlund was instrumental in developing inquiry activities.

ELL Consultant

JIM CUMMINS, Ph.D.

Professor and Canada Research Chair,
Curriculum, Teaching and Learning
Department at the University of Toronto
Dr. Cummins's research focuses on literacy development in multilingual schools and the role technology plays in learning across the curriculum. *Interactive Science* incorporates research-based principles for integrating language with the teaching of academic content based on Dr. Cummins's work.

Program Consultants

WILLIAM BROZO, Ph.D.

Professor of Literacy,
Graduate School of Education,
George Mason University,
Fairfax, Virginia
Dr. Brozo is the author of numerous articles and books on literacy development. He coauthors a column in *The Reading Teacher* and serves on the editorial review board of the *Journal of Adolescent & Adult Literacy.*

KRISTI ZENCHAK, M.S.

Biology Instructor,
Oakton Community College,
Des Plaines, Illinois
Kristi Zenchak helps elementary teachers incorporate science, technology, engineering, and math activities into the classroom. STEM activities that produce viable solutions to real-world problems not only motivate students but also prepare students for future STEM careers. Ms. Zenchak helps elementary teachers understand the basic science concepts and provides STEM activities that are easy to implement in the classroom.

Content Reviewers

Brian Ancell, Assistant Professor
Department of Geosciences
Texas Tech University
Lubbock, Texas

D. Brent Burt, Professor
Department of Biology
Stephen F. Austin State University
Nacogdoches, Texas

Gerald B. Cleaver, Ph.D.
Department of Physics
Baylor University
Waco, Texas

David Lamp
Associate Professor of Physics/Education
Texas Tech University
Lubbock, Texas

Dr. Richard H. Langley
Department of Chemistry
Stephen F. Austin State University
Nacogdoches, Texas

Heidi Marcum
Department of Environmental Science
Baylor University
Waco, Texas

Emilia Morosan
Rice University
Houston, Texas

Aaron S. Yoshinobu, Ph.D
Associate Professor
Department of Geosciences
Texas Tech University
Lubbock, Texas

Built for Texas

Texas Interactive Science covers 100% of the Texas Essential Knowledge and Skills for Science. Built on feedback from Texas educators, *Texas Interactive Science* focuses on what is important to Texas teachers and students, and creates a personal, relevant, and engaging classroom experience.

Pearson would like to extend a special thank you to all of the teachers from across the state of Texas who helped guide the development of this program.

Unit A
Science, Engineering, and Technology

Lab zone®

Inquiry Warm-Up
How do you use your senses to identify objects? . . . 4

Quick Lab
What questions can you ask about the world around you?. 7
How can you observe objects?. 15
Why do scientists use tools?. 21
How do scientists answer questions? 31
What are some ways to record and share data? 37

Lab Investigation
How do you know the mass of objects? 42

Open-Ended Inquiry
What do pill bugs need? . . . 54

These scientists work at Johnson Space Center in Houston, Texas.

Texas

Chapter 1
The Nature of Science

PEARSON Texas.com

Unit B
Physical Science

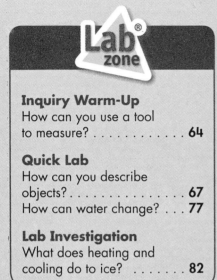

Lab zone

Inquiry Warm-Up
How can you use a tool
to measure? **64**

Quick Lab
How can you describe
objects? **67**
How can water change? . . . **77**

Lab Investigation
What does heating and
cooling do to ice? **82**

*The hot air balloons at the
festival in Plano, Texas, have
many shapes and colors.*

STEM Project
Go online to find the project for
this chapter. You will design and
test a window shade.

Texas

Chapter 2

Matter

PEARSON Texas.com

Unit B
Physical Science

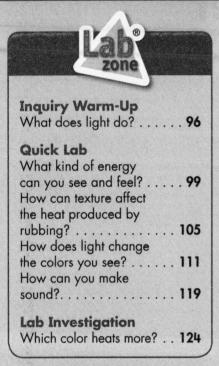

Inquiry Warm-Up
What does light do? 96

Quick Lab
What kind of energy
can you see and feel? 99
How can texture affect
the heat produced by
rubbing? 105
How does light change
the colors you see? 111
How can you make
sound? 119

Lab Investigation
Which color heats more? . . 124

*Reunion Tower in Dallas, Texas,
uses light energy at night.*

STEM Project

Go online to find the project
for this chapter. You will make
a periscope.

viii

Texas

Chapter

3

Energy

PEARSON Texas.com

Unit B
Physical Science

Texas

Chapter 4

Movement

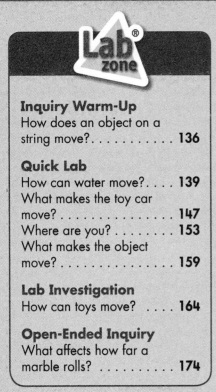

The roller coaster at Six Flags® Over Texas moves at a very fast speed.

STEM Project

Go online to find the project for this chapter. You will build a tool using magnets to reach far-away objects.

PEARSON Texas.com

Unit C
Earth Science

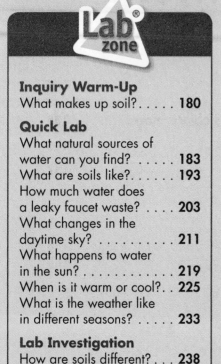

Inquiry Warm-Up
What makes up soil?..... 180

Quick Lab
What natural sources of
water can you find? 183
What are soils like?...... 193
How much water does
a leaky faucet waste? 203
What changes in the
daytime sky? 211
What happens to water
in the sun? 219
When is it warm or cool?.. 225
What is the weather like
in different seasons? 233

Lab Investigation
How are soils different?.... 238

Open-Ended Inquiry
How can you see the
wind blow? 250

*Palo Duro Canyon has colorful
rocks and soil.*

S T E M Project
Go online to find the project for
this chapter. You will design and
test a simple rain gauge.

x

Earth, Sky, and Weather

PEARSON Texas.com

Unit D
Life Science

Inquiry Warm-Up
How are flowers alike and different? **256**

Quick Lab
Which is a living thing? . . . **259**
Do plants need water? **265**
How do leaves compare? . . **277**
How do animals change? . . **283**
How are babies and parents alike and different? **291**
What do living things eat? . . **297**

Lab Investigation
How can you model a food chain? **304**

The prickly pear cactus is the state plant of Texas.

S T E M Project
Go online to find the project for this chapter. You will build a compost pile.

Texas
Chapter 6
Plants and Animals

PEARSON Texas.com

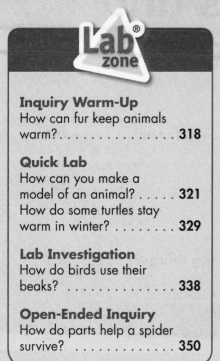

*Bighorn sheep use their horns
to scrape the sharp spines off
cactus.*

STEM Project

Go online to find the project
for this chapter. You will build
a greenhouse.

Texas

Chapter 7

Living Things and Their Environments

PEARSON Texas.com

Engage with the Page!

Untamed Science videos make learning science fun at the beginning of every chapter.

This is your book. You can write in it. Connect and interact as you read the Texas Interactive Science write-in student edition.

Where does the soil come from?

Earth, Sky, and Weather

Texas

Chapter 5

Lesson 1 What is on Earth?

Lesson 2 What are rocks and soil?

Lesson 3 How do people use natural resources?

Lesson 4 What causes day and night?

Lesson 5 What is the water cycle?

Lesson 6 How can you measure weather?

Lesson 7 What are the four seasons?

Pearson Flipped Videos for Science give you another way to learn and review every lesson!

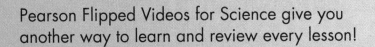

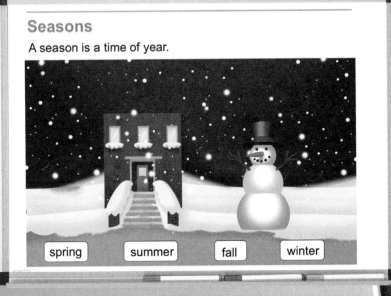

Get active with science with whiteboard-ready activities.

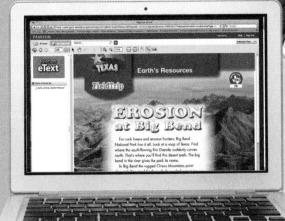

Access all print program resources in English or Spanish at PEARSONTexas.com.

Connect what you do to what you read and see.

Be a Scientist!

Engage with science through hands-on activities in each lesson! With easy-to-find materials, these activities can be conducted in the classroom or at home!

Start Each Chapter

Inquiry Warm-Up
TEKS 10B, 2B, 2C, 4A

How are flowers alike and different?

☐ 1. Take a flower apart.

☐ 2. Classify   Group the parts that are alike.

☐ 3. Observe   Compare the parts that are different.

Explain Your Results

4. Communicate   How are the parts alike?

5. How are the parts different?

Materials

hand lens

paper

different flowers

Inquiry Skill
Classify means to sort things into groups that are alike and different.

256

Quick Lab
TEKS 2D, 2E, 9A

Do plants need water?

☐ 1. Observe the plant. Add water.

☐ 2. Predict what will happen.

☐ 3. Wait 1 day. Record your observation.

Explain Your Results

4. Predict   What will happen if you do not water the plant anymore?

Materials

plant   water

265

Start Each Lesson

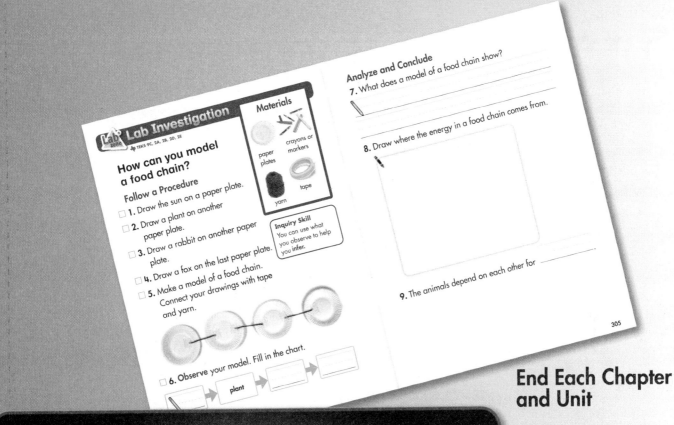

Lab Investigation
TEKS 9C, 2A, 2B, 2D, 2E

How can you model a food chain?

Follow a Procedure

☐ **1.** Draw the sun on a paper plate.

☐ **2.** Draw a plant on another paper plate.

☐ **3.** Draw a rabbit on another paper plate.

☐ **4.** Draw a fox on the last paper plate.

☐ **5.** Make a model of a food chain. Connect your drawings with tape and yarn.

☐ **6.** Observe your model. Fill in the chart.

plant

Materials

paper plates

crayons or markers

yarn

tape

Inquiry Skill
You can use what you observe to help you infer.

Analyze and Conclude

7. What does a model of a food chain show?

8. Draw where the energy in a food chain comes from.

9. The animals depend on each other for

305

End Each Chapter and Unit

Which bird beak can crush seeds?

00:07 / 00:38

1 of 2

At PEARSONTexas.com go online and conduct labs virtually! No goggles and no mess.

Have Fun!

Show What You Know!

Start Each Chapter

Focus on the **TEKS** with big questions.

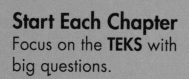

How are living things like their parents?

I will know TEKS 10C
I will know that plants and animals look like their parents. (Also 2D, 2B)

Vocabulary
parent

Connect to Math

Marta's dog Molly had 7 puppies. Two of them are white. The rest are brown. Circle the number sentence that shows how many brown puppies Molly has.

Math TEKS 3D

7 – 2 = 5 brown puppies

7 + 2 = 9 brown puppies

PEARSONTexas.com

290

Start Each Lesson

One or more **TEKS** are highlighted in a student-friendly and easy-to-understand way!

After reading small chunks of information, stop to check for understanding of the **TEKS**.

Chicken Life Cycle

Living things grow and change.
A **life cycle** is the way a living thing grows and changes.
A chicken is an animal.
Chickens go through a life cycle.
The chicken begins as an egg.
The egg will hatch.
Hatch means to come out of an egg.

Observe the pictures. **Write** numbers to show the order of the chicken life cycle.

egg

A chick comes out of the egg.
A chick is a young chicken.
The chick grows and changes.
It becomes an adult chicken.
The adult chicken may lay eggs.
The life cycle begins again.

Compare and Contrast Tell how a chick and chicken are alike and different.

chicken

chick

Apply content to new situations from Texas and beyond.

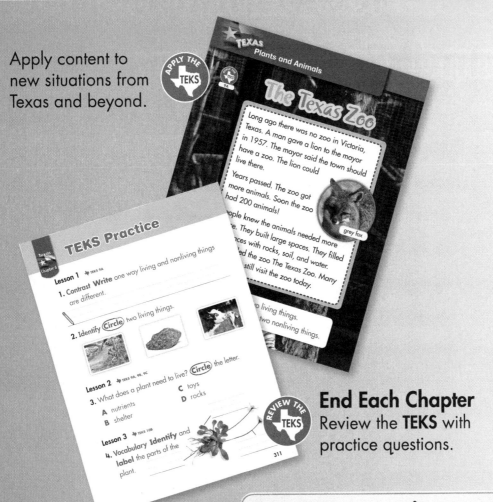

End Each Chapter
Review the **TEKS** with practice questions.

See what you already know.

Check what you know at the end of each lesson and chapter.

Get More Practice on skills and/or content, based on your performance.

Predict your exam readiness with unit-level benchmark assessments.

Get extra practice instantly online!

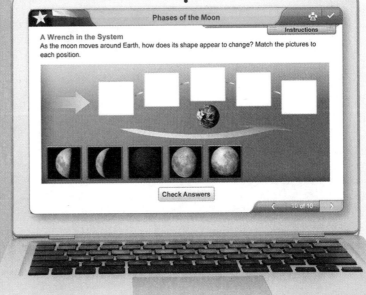

Track Your Learning Online.

Science, Engineering, and Technology

1

How are you a **scientist** when you bake?

The Nature of Science

 FOCUS ON TEKS

3C

What do scientists do?

Circle a tool bakers use.

 Texas Essential Knowledge and Skills

TEKS 1A Recognize and demonstrate safe practices as described in the Texas Safety Standards during classroom and outdoor investigations, including wearing safety goggles, washing hands, and using materials appropriately. **2A** Ask questions about organisms, objects, and events observed in the natural world. **2C** Collect data and make observations using simple equipment such as hand lenses, primary balances, and non-standard measurement tools. **2D** Record and organize data using pictures, numbers, and words. **2E** Communicate observations and provide reasons for explanations using student-generated data from simple descriptive investigations. **3C** Describe what scientists do. **4A** Collect, record, and compare information using tools, including computers, hand lenses, primary balances, cups, bowls, magnets, collecting nets, notebooks, and safety goggles; timing devices, including clocks and timers; non-standard measuring items such as paper clips and clothespins; weather instruments such as classroom demonstration thermometers and wind socks; and materials to support observations of habitats of organisms such as aquariums and terrariums.
Process TEKS: 1B, 2B, 3A, 3B, 4B

TEKS 2E, 5A

How do you use your senses to identify objects?

Scientists observe to find out about objects.

Materials

sock with object inside

crayons

☑ **1. Observe** Feel the object in the sock. Do not look! Is it heavy? Is it soft?

☑ **2. Record** what it feels like.

Inquiry Skill
You can use what you observe to help you **infer.**

☑ **3. Infer** Draw the object.

Explain Your Results

4. Look at the object.
    What do you see that you did not feel?

Focus on Picture Clues

You will practice the reading strategy **picture clues** in this chapter. Pictures can give you clues about what you read.

At the Vet

The dog is at the vet. The vet helps the dog stay healthy.

Practice It!

Look for clues in the picture. **Write** how you know the dog stays healthy.

At the Vet

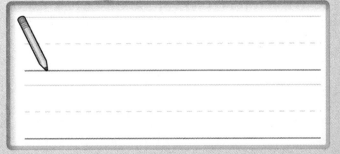

The dog is at the vet.

Clue

Clue

What questions do scientists ask?

I will know TEKS 2A, 3C
I will know that scientists ask questions about the world.
(Also **1B**, **2B**, **2D**, and **2E**)

Vocabulary
inquiry

Connect to Reading

Scientists are always asking questions. Write one question you have about the world around you. ➜ ELA TEKS 23A

TEKS 2A, 2B, 2D, 2E

What questions can you ask about the world around you?

☐ **1.** Look out the window.

☐ **2. Observe** What do you see? Draw a picture.

☐ **3.** Write a question you have about what you see.

Explain Your Results

4. Communicate Share your question with a partner.

Scientists

Scientists are people who study the world around them.

Scientists ask questions.

Picture Clues Tell two questions the girl in the picture might ask.

The boy is a scientist. He is studying what is in the jar.

The girl is using a tool to observe.

8

The boy looks in a book for answers.

The children are doing an experiment to answer their question.

Scientists answer questions too.

Scientists use inquiry.

Inquiry means looking for answers.

Underline the ways scientists can find answers to their questions.

Questions

Scientists ask questions about many things.
Scientists ask questions about animals.
Scientists ask questions about plants.
Scientists ask questions about rocks
and soil.
Scientists ask questions about weather too.
Write a question you might ask about
this storm.

Lab zone Quick Lab

Science Questions
Work with a partner.
Make a list of science
questions about
plants, rocks, or the
weather. Discuss why
the questions are
science questions.

TEKS 2A

Discovery

Scientists make discoveries.

A discovery is a new thing or idea.

Discoveries can change our lives.

The discovery of germs changed the way people act.

Doctors did not always wash their hands with soap.

People would get germs from the doctor.

Now doctors wash their hands with soap.

The soap gets rid of germs.

Their tools are washed with soap too.

Doctors do not pass germs to others.

Circle something scientists do. **Tell** about a discovery.

Dr. John C. Pérez

Dr. John C. Pérez is a scientist. He asks questions. He works with other scientists.

He studies snakes. He uses tools to help him. Microscopes and test tubes are some of his tools.

This snake lives outdoors.

Never touch a snake. They can be dangerous! Dr. Pérez knows how to be careful with snakes. He keeps snakes in his lab where he can observe them safely.

He is a teacher in Kingsville, Texas. He still studies snakes. He still asks questions.

Tell how you know Dr. Pérez is a scientist.

13

What skills do scientists use?

 I will know TEKS 2C, 3C
I will know the skills scientists use to learn about new things. (Also **2B**, **4A**, **5A**, and **2D**)

Vocabulary
observe

Connect to
Reading

Look around. What do you see? Close your eyes. What do you smell? What do you hear? Write about it. ELA TEKS 19A

🔺 TEKS 2C, 2D, 4A, 5A

How can you observe objects?

☐ **1.** Look at a feather.
Observe it with a hand lens.
Draw what you see.

Materials

feather

crayons or markers

hand lens

☑ **2.** Feel the feather. Tell what you learn.

Explain Your Results

3. How did the hand lens help you **observe**?

_____

_____

_____

15

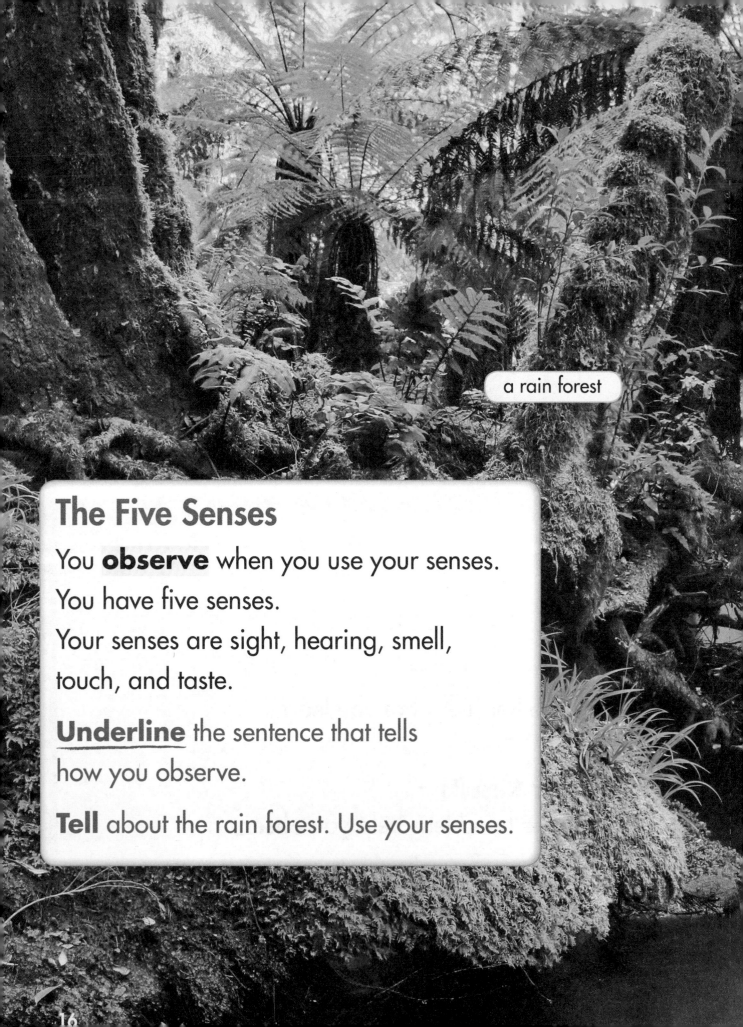

a rain forest

The Five Senses

You **observe** when you use your senses.
You have five senses.
Your senses are sight, hearing, smell,
touch, and taste.

Underline the sentence that tells
how you observe.

Tell about the rain forest. Use your senses.

This tree frog lives in the rain forest.

You can observe color with your sense of sight.
You can observe size and shape with your senses of sight and touch.

Picture Clues Write one thing you observe about the frog in the picture.

Observe and Predict

You observe things.

You use what you observe to predict.

Predict means to tell what might happen next.

Suppose you observe that danger is near.

You can predict what the fish will do.

You might predict the fish will swim away.

Picture Clues Look at the fish.

Tell about their size, shape, and color.

Predict what this fish
will do when it gets hungry.

Compare and Classify

You share what you observe with others.

You compare what you observe. You can compare how things are alike. You also talk about how things are different.

You classify things too. You classify when you group things by how they are alike. You can classify the fish by color.

Tell a partner how the fish are alike.

 Quick Lab

Classify Objects
Gather ten small objects. Observe them. Make a chart to classify them by shape, color, and texture. **TEKS 5A**

How do scientists use tools?

 I will know TEKS **1A, 1B, 4A, 4B** I will know how to use some science tools. I will know how to do science safely. (Also **2C**, **2D**, and **2E**.)

Vocabulary
tool
measure
safety

Connect to
Math

Math TEKS 5D

Jack and Sam each find a leaf. Jack measures his leaf with a ruler. It is 6 centimeters long. Sam uses a ruler too. Her leaf is 9 centimeters long. How much longer is Sam's leaf?

9 − 6 = _____

TEKS 2C, 2D, 2E, 4A, 4B

Materials

paper clips

metric ruler

Why do scientists use tools?

☐ **1.** Pick an object. Use a metric ruler to **measure** its length in centimeters. **Record.**

☐ **2.** Use paper clips to measure the object. Record its length in paper clips.

Object Length

Object Length	
Length in centimeters	
Length in paper clips	

Explain Your Results

3. Compare the results. Why do you need more centimeters than paper clips to measure the object?

_____

_____

_____

_____

4. Think about the two ways you **measured.** Why might scientists use a metric ruler and not paper clips?

_____

_____

_____

_____

21

Tools

Scientists use many different tools.
A **tool** is something that makes
work easier.

You can use tools to observe.

Underline what makes work easier.

You can use a hand lens to make things look larger.

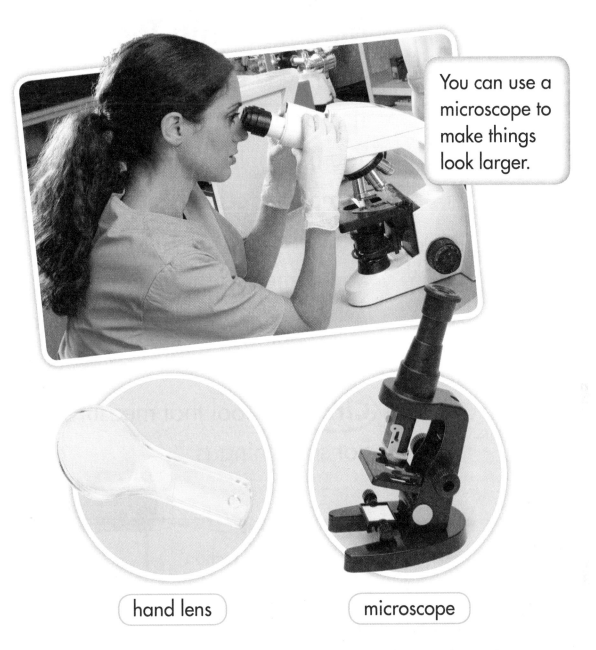

You can use a microscope to make things look larger.

hand lens

microscope

A hand lens is a tool.

A hand lens makes objects look bigger.

A microscope makes objects look bigger too.

You can see small things with a microscope.

You cannot see these things with just your eyes.

Draw an X on the tool that helps you
see things you cannot see with just your eyes.

A **thermometer** measures temperature. Temperature is how hot or cold something is. This thermometer tells temperature in degrees Fahrenheit and Celsius.

Measure with Tools

When you **measure** you learn the size or amount of something. You use tools to measure. Sometimes scientists do not measure. Sometimes scientists estimate. An estimate is a careful guess about the size or amount of something.

Circle the tool that measures how hot something is.

A **wind sock** shows the direction of the wind.

 Quick Lab

Measure Temperature
Use a thermometer. Measure the temperature in your classroom every day for 5 days. Record your results. Compare the results. 🔺 TEKS 2C, 4A

A **pan balance** measures how much mass an object has. Objects that have a lot of mass feel heavy. Objects that do not have a lot of mass feel light.

A **clock** measures time.

A **timer** measures how long something takes.

A **measuring cup** measures volume. Volume is how much space something takes up.

You can use **paper clips** or **clothespins** to measure. They can measure how long something is.

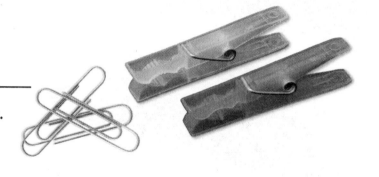

A **ruler** measures how long something is. This ruler measures in inches and centimeters.

Choose a tool to measure how long your shoe is.

Write what it measures in inches and centimeters.

25

More Tools

Some tools help keep you safe.

Some tools help you collect information.

Some tools help you record information.

You can use **magnets** to attract some metals.

You can use a **computer** to find information. You can record information on a computer too.

You can write observations in a **notebook.** You can draw them too.

Safety goggles protect your eyes.

Circle the tools that you can use to record information.

Draw something you could gather in a collecting net.

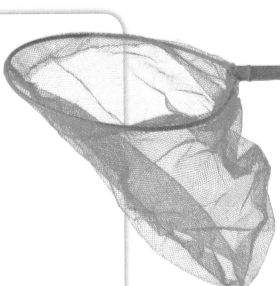

You can gather things with a **collecting net.**

You can observe animals and plants in an **aquarium.**

You can observe animals and plants in a **terrarium.**

Tell about a tool you could use to observe the aquarium and terrarium.

Safety in Science

Safety means staying out of danger.
Follow these safety rules indoors and outdoors when you do activities. These rules keep you and others safe and healthy.

1. Use materials appropriately.

2. Wear safety goggles when needed.

3. Tell your teacher immediately about accidents.

4. Wash your hands well after each activity.

Tell how these rules keep you and others safe and healthy.

The girl washes her hands with soap and water.

Picture Clues Tell how the girl stays safe.

Tie your hair back if it is long.

Wear safety goggles when needed.

Wear gloves to keep your hands safe.

Handle scissors and other equipment carefully.

Clean up spills immediately.

Wear shoes without open ends.

You spill water on the floor.

Circle the rule that you should follow.

Write why it is important to follow safety rules.

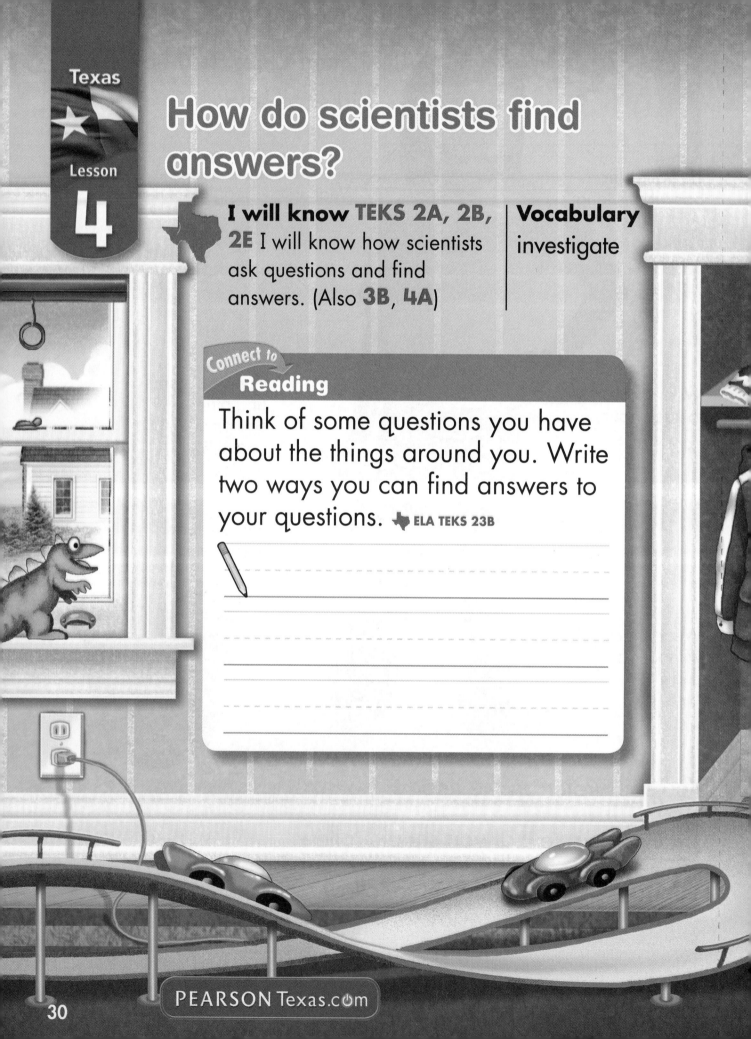

How do scientists find answers?

I will know TEKS 2A, 2B, 2E I will know how scientists ask questions and find answers. (Also 3B, 4A)

Vocabulary
investigate

Connect to Reading

Think of some questions you have about the things around you. Write two ways you can find answers to your questions. ELA TEKS 23B

Materials

black paper

timer

How do scientists answer questions?

☐ Think about the following question.
Can sunlight warm an object?

☐ **1. Observe** a piece of paper.
Feel it. It is **(warm/cool)**.

☐ **2.** Make a **prediction.**
The paper will get **(warm/cool)** in sunlight.

☐ **3.** Test your prediction.
Put the paper in sunlight.
Wait 15 minutes.
The paper got **(warm/cool)**.

Explain Your Results

4. Draw a Conclusion
Can sunlight warm objects?
Tell how you know.

Science Inquiry

You ask questions when you do science.
You investigate to find answers.
To **investigate** is to look for answers to questions.

(Circle) the word that means to look for answers to questions.

Picture Clues Look at the picture.
Ask a question the scientist might ask about plants.

This scientist investigates plants.

This scientist observes the rhinoceros.

Scientists have ways to investigate. They follow steps when they do experiments.

Write what the scientist might write in the notebook.

Scientific Investigation and Reasoning

Ask a question.

Ask a question that you want answered.
How does sunlight change the way plants grow?

Make your hypothesis.

Tell what you think might be the answer to your question.

If a plant is moved away from sunlight, then it will grow toward the sunlight because plants need light.

Plan a fair test.

Change only one thing.
Keep everything else the same.
Move one plant away from the window.

Tell another hypothesis.

Do your test.

Test your hypothesis.

Do your test more than once.

Observe the results of your test.

See if your results are the same.

Collect and record your data.

Keep records of what you find.

Use words or drawings to help.

Draw a conclusion.

Decide if your observations match your hypothesis.

Tell what you decide.

Compare your conclusion with a partner's conclusion.

Moving Objects

Think of ways to make objects move. Try your ideas. Record the different ways. Compare your results with a partner. **TEKS 2B**

The boy draws a picture to keep records.

Picture Clues Write how sunlight changes the way plants grow.

Tell how you know.

How do scientists share data?

 I will know TEKS 2D, 2E, 3B I will know how scientists share the data they collect.

Vocabulary
data
record

Connect to

Math

Math TEKS 8C

Mr. Smith's class observed the weather for 12 days. They made a chart to record the data.

Weather

What can you tell from looking at the chart?

_____

_____

_____

Quick Lab

TEKS 2D, 3B

What are some ways to record and share data?

☐ **1.** Predict how many cups you can stack. **Record** your prediction.

☐ **2.** Stack the cups as high as you can. Make a tally mark each time you add a cup.

Trial	Prediction	Number of Cups	Total
1			
2			
3			
4			

☐ **3. Record** the total using a number.

☐ **4.** Repeat 3 more times.

Explain Your Results

5. Compare data with others. Tell any pattern you find. Predict the number of cups you could stack in trial 5.

6. You **recorded data** in two ways. How else could you have recorded data?

_____

_____

Data

You collect information when you do science.
This information is called **data.**

You can use your senses to collect data.

Write what you observe about the dog.

You can use pictures and words to show what you observe. You can use numbers too.

Picture Clues **Draw** the data that the girl in the picture might draw.

Record Data

You **record** when you write or draw what you learn.

A chart is a way to record data.

Ask five people if they like a cat, a dog, or a bird best.

Fill in a square in the chart next to the animals your classmates choose.

Favorite Animals

cat					
dog					
bird					

Lab zone Quick Lab

Favorite Pet Name
Think of three pet names. Ask six people which name they like best. Make a chart to record their choices. TEKS 2D

Show Data

You can use charts to show data.
You can also use graphs.
Use your data to make a
picture graph.

Count the votes for each pet.

Draw one animal for each vote.

Favorite Animals

Pet		1	2	3	4	5
	cat					
	dog					
	bird					

Number of votes

Write a conclusion from your data.

_____

_____

_____

_____

TEKS 1A, 2C, 2D, 2E, 4A, 5A

How do you know the mass of objects?

Follow a Procedure

☐ **1. Measure** how heavy the cup is.
First, put the cup on one side of a balance.
Next, slowly add gram cubes to the other side.
Then stop when the balance is level.
Last, **record** the number of cubes.

☐ **2.** Measure how heavy 10 beans are. Record.

☐ **3.** Measure how heavy the cup is with the 10 beans inside. Record.

Materials

plastic cup

10 beans

balance

gram cubes

Inquiry Skill
Scientists observe what happens and **record** their results.

Texas Safety
LAB RULES
Use materials correctly.

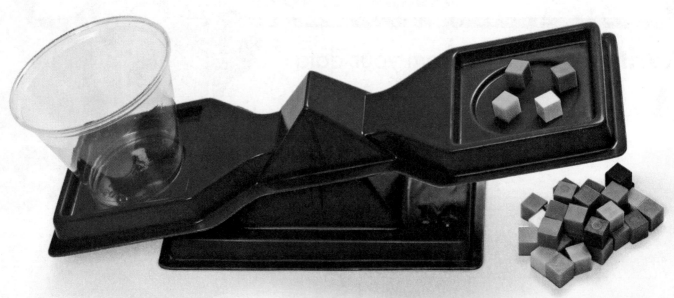

Number of Cubes to Balance

Object	Number of Cubes
Cup	
10 beans	
Cup with 10 beans	

Analyze and Conclude

4. Look at your data.

Add the numbers for the cup and the beans.

_____ cubes + _____ cubes = _____ cubes

(cup)   (beans)   (cup with 10 beans)

5. Which is heavier?

cup   10 beans

6. Draw a Conclusion How can you use a pan balance to find out which object is heavier or lighter?

_____

_____

_____

_____

APPLY THE TEKS

3C

Johnson Space Center

Scientists work together at the center.

You can visit Johnson Space Center in Houston, Texas. Many scientists work there. They study outer space. They study Mars. They want to know how astronauts can visit Mars. They study food. They want to know what foods are healthy for astronauts. They study plants too. They want to know how plants can grow in space. The scientists are very busy.

Underline what scientists do at Johnson Space Center.

Vocabulary Smart Cards

data
inquiry
investigate
measure
observe
record
safety
tool

Play a Game!

Cut out the cards.

Work with a partner.

Pick a card.

Act out the word.

Have your partner guess the word.

measure
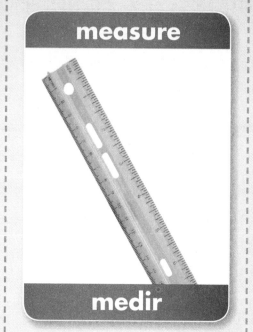
medir

inquiry

indagación

safety

seguridad

observe

observar

investigate

investigar

tool

instrumento

looking for answers

buscar respuestas

to use a tool to find the size or amount of something

usar un instrumento para saber el tamaño o la cantidad de algo

when you use your senses

cuando usas tus sentidos

staying out of danger

estar fuera de peligro

something that makes work easier

algo que hace más fácil el trabajo

to look for answers to questions

buscar respuestas a las preguntas

 46

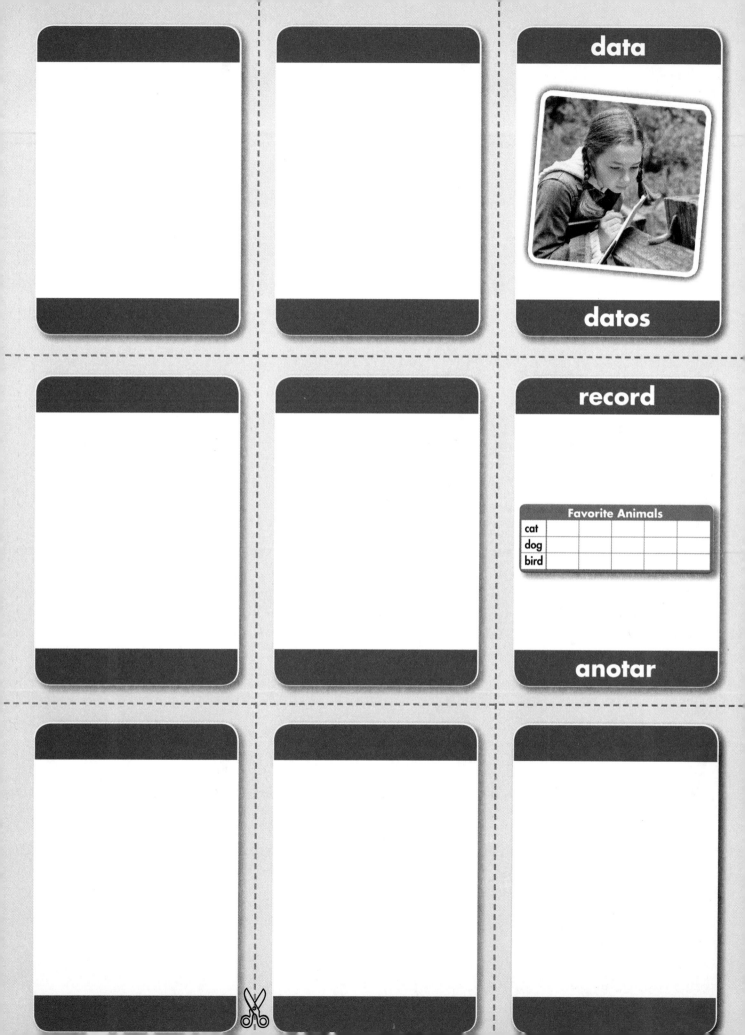

data

datos

record

Favorite Animals

cat				
dog				
bird				

anotar

information you
collect

información que
reúnes

when scientists write
or draw what they
learn

cuando los científicos
escriben o dibujan lo
que descubren

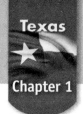
TEKS Practice

Lesson 1 TEKS 2A, 3C

1. Vocabulary What is inquiry?

_____

2. Apply Some scientists ask questions about weather. **Write** a question you have about weather.

_____

_____

_____

Lesson 2 TEKS 3C

3. Compare (Circle) the scientist who listens to observe.

Lesson 3 TEKS 1A, 1B, 4A

4. Picture Clues Write how the children stay safe.

_____

_____

TEKS Practice

5. Apply Why do scientists follow safety rules?

Lesson 4 🖐 TEKS 2A, 2B, 3C

6. Vocabulary Write what scientists do when they investigate.

Lesson 5 🖐 TEKS 2D, 2E

7. What do scientists use to keep records?
Circle the letter.

A words and pictures   **C** safety

B tools such as saws   **D** scientific methods

TEKS Practice

Chapter 1

Lesson 1 What questions do scientists ask?

TEKS: 2A, 3C

Lesson 2 What skills do scientists use?

TEKS: 3C

Lesson 3 How do scientists use tools?

TEKS: 1A, 1B, 4A

Lesson 4 How do scientists find answers?

TEKS: 2A, 2B, 3C

Lesson 5 How do scientists share data?

TEKS: 2D, 2E

★ TEKS Practice: Chapter Review

Read each question and circle the best answer.

1 Which tool can you use to measure temperature?

A Pan balance

B Ruler

C Thermometer

D Hand lens

2 Which question is a science question about a rock?

F How much did it cost?

G Is it smooth or rough?

H Who found it?

J Is it pretty?

3 Daniel wants to know how a caterpillar moves. What might he do to find out?

A Feel the caterpillar

B Measure the caterpillar

C Listen to the caterpillar

D Observe the caterpillar

4 Natalie spills water on the floor. Why is it important to clean up the spill right away?

   F Someone could fall down and get hurt.

   G The classroom must look nice.

   H We must not waste water.

   J Water has germs.

---

5 How does a scientist begin an investigation?

   A By observing the results of a test

   B By drawing a conclusion

   C By making a hypothesis

   D By asking a question

If you have trouble with . . .					
Question	1	2	3	4	5
See chapter (lesson)	1 (3)	1 (1)	1 (2)	1 (3)	1 (4)
TEKS	2C	2A	2B	1B	2A

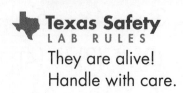
🔻 **TEKS 1A, 2B, 2C, 2D, 2E, 3A, 4A, 9A, 9B**

What do pill bugs need?

All pets need habitats. A habitat is a place a plant or animal lives. A friend gives you pet pill bugs. Pill bugs are living things. They have needs. You must design a habitat for them. What will your pill bugs need?

Find a problem.

☑ **1.** How will you meet each need?

Pill Bug Needs Chart	
Need	**How Will I Meet the Need**
Air	
Shelter	
Food (energy)	
Water	

🔻 **Texas Safety**
L A B   R U L E S
They are alive!
Handle with care.

Plan and draw.

☐ **2.** List the steps to build the habitat.

_____

_____

_____

_____

_____

☐ **3.** Draw your **design.**
You will use the materials on the next page.

Choose materials.

☐ **4.** Circle the materials you will use.

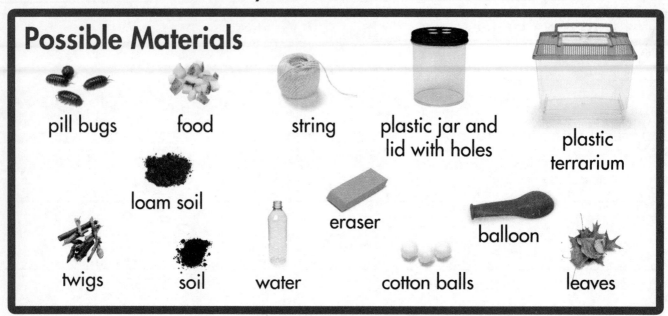

Possible Materials

pill bugs food string plastic jar and lid with holes plastic terrarium

loam soil

eraser

balloon

twigs soil water cotton balls leaves

☐ **5.** Tell which need each material meets.

Make and test.

☐ **6.** Make the habitat you **designed.**
Follow your plan.

☐ **7.** Draw your pill bugs in the habitat.

Record and share.

☑ **8. Observe** your design for one week.
Observe the habitat.
Observe the pill bugs.

Day Observations

Day	Observation
1	
2	
3	
4	
5	

These pill bugs are shown
five times their regular size.

☐ **9.** Compare your habitat with other groups.
How were the habitats the same?

_____

_____

_____

_____

☐ **10.** How were the habitats different?

_____

_____

_____

_____

☐ **11.** How could you **redesign** your pill bug habitat?

_____

_____

_____

_____

Physical Science

 Texas Essential Knowledge and Skills

Content TEKS
Matter: 5A, 5B
Energy: 6A, 8D
Movement: 6B, 6C, 6D

Process TEKS
1A, 2A, 2B, 2C, 2D, 2E, 3B, 4A, 4B

Why do statues keep their shapes?

Matter

Lesson 1 What is matter?

Lesson 2 What are solids, liquids, and gases?

 How can you describe matter?

Tell about the horses.

 Texas Essential Knowledge and Skills

TEKS 5A Classify objects by observable properties of the materials from which they are made such as larger and smaller, heavier and lighter, shape, color, and texture. **5B** Predict and identify changes in materials caused by heating and cooling such as ice melting, water freezing, and water evaporating.
Process TEKS: 1A, 2C, 2D, 2E, 3B, 4A, 4B

How can you use a tool to measure?

Materials

Straw Ruler B

Straw Ruler A

☑ **1.** Use Straw Ruler A.

Measure the width of your desk. How many straw pieces wide is it? **Record.** Measure 3 more things.

Inquiry Skill
You can **estimate** before you measure.

☑ **2.** Use Straw Ruler B. Measure each thing again. Record.

What I Measured	Measured Using Straw Ruler A	Measured Using Straw Ruler B

Explain Your Results

3. Infer Why were your **measurements** different?

_____

_____

4. Why measure with the same size unit?

_____

_____

_____

Focus on **Main Idea and Details**

You will practice the reading strategy **main idea and details** in this chapter.
The main idea is what the sentences are about.
Details tell about the main idea.

A Clay Cat

The object is a clay cat.
The ears are blue triangles.
The whiskers are long and yellow.

Practice It!

Write two details that tell about the main idea.

The object is a clay cat.

Main Idea

Detail	**Detail**

What is matter?

I will know TEKS 5A
I will know how to describe matter. I will know how to classify matter. (Also **2C**, **2D**, **4A**, and **4B**)

Vocabulary
matter
mass
weight

Connect to Math

Math TEKS 8A

Look around the room. Find objects that are blue, red, or yellow. Record the number in the tally chart.

Blue	Red	Yellow

Quick Lab

TEKS 5A, 2D

How can you describe objects?

☐ **1.** Choose two objects. **Observe** them. Use your senses.

☐ **2. Record** your observations in the chart.

	Color	Size	Shape	Weight	Texture
Object					
Object					

Explain Your Results

3. How are the two objects alike?

_____

_____

4. What is another object you could group with these objects? Why?

_____

_____

Matter

Matter is anything that takes up space.

Matter has mass.

Mass is the amount of matter in an object.

The table is matter and has mass.

Main Idea and Details

Underline two details about matter.

The table has more mass than the glue bottle.

Everything around you is made of matter. All the things in the classroom are made of matter. Even the air you breathe is matter!

Draw another object in the classroom. **Tell** about it.

Objects and Matter

All objects are made of matter.
You can describe objects many ways.
Objects can be different colors.
Objects can be different
sizes and shapes.
Objects can be hard or soft.
The red marble is round and hard.

Label the objects.

square   purple   small   large

Draw an ✗ on
two soft objects.

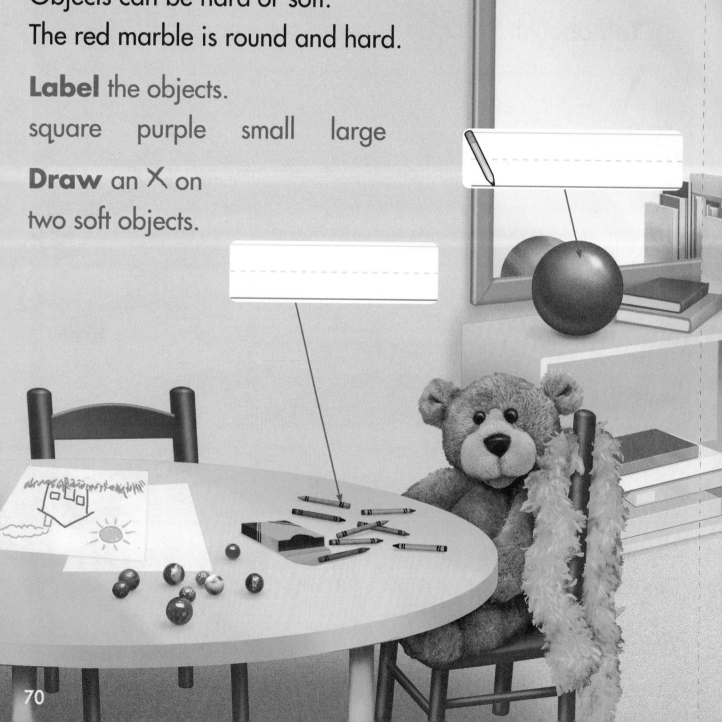

Describe and Group Objects

Objects can feel different.
The wall feels smooth.
Objects can be heavy or light.
Weight is how heavy an object is.
The books are heavy.

You can group objects by how
they are alike.
The balls and marbles are alike.
The balls and marbles are round.

Tell how you can sort the objects in the room by color.

Compare the orange ball and the softball. **Tell** which ball is heavier and which is lighter. **Tell** which object has the greater mass.

More Ways to Describe Objects

Objects can float or sink.

Float means to stay on top of a liquid.

Sink means to fall to the bottom of a liquid.

Lemonade is a liquid.

The ice cubes float in the lemonade.

Objects can be different temperatures.

The lemonade is cold.

Objects can be made of different materials.

The sink is metal.

The timer is plastic.

Draw an X on something that sinks.

Circle something that is hot.

Measure

Use paper clips to measure your desk. How wide is it? How long is it? Record and compare the numbers. Do the same thing using clothespins. Which measurement is larger? Why?

TEKS 4A, 4B

Write two words that describe the lemonade.

73

The Plano Balloon Festival

APPLY THE TEKS 5A

Plano, Texas, has a balloon festival every year. Many people come to watch.

The balloons at the festival have burners, or fires. The burners make the air hot inside the balloon. Hot air makes the balloons rise.

The balloons go up at night too. You can see them glow in the sky!

There are many balloons at the festival. They have many shapes and colors.

They have contests too. There is a big target on the ground. Pilots fly balloons over the target. The pilots try to drop beanbags on the target. It is harder than it sounds!

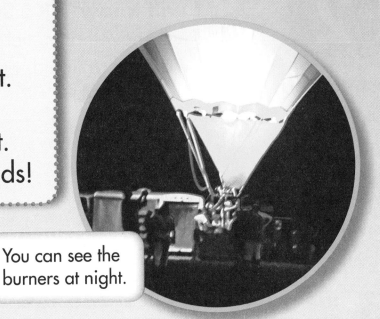

You can see the burners at night.

Write why heat is important for hot air balloons.

Describe the hot air balloons. Tell about their size, color, and shape.

75

What are solids, liquids, and gases?

I will know TEKS 5B
I will know that matter can be a solid, a liquid, or a gas. (Also **1A**, **4A**)

Vocabulary
solid
liquid
gas
freeze
melt
evaporate

Connect to
Reading

A solid has its own shape. Find a solid in the classroom. Tell how you know it is a solid. **ELA TEKS 28**

TEKS 5B, 1A, 4A

How can water change?

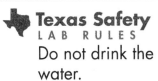
☐ **1.** Put water in a cup. Ask your teacher to mark the water line.

☐ **2.** Put the cup in a freezer. Wait 1 day. **Predict.**

☐ **3.** Compare the mark to the ice.

☐ **4.** Leave the cup out. **Observe** each day for 1 week. **Identify.**

Texas Safety
LAB RULES
Do not drink the water.

Do not put the cup back into the freezer.

Explain Your Results

5. Communicate What happens to the water over time?

Solids

Matter can be a solid, liquid, or gas.

A **solid** has its own shape.

A solid has its own size.

A solid does not change shape
when it is moved.

The box is a solid.
The toys are solids.

Main Idea and Details

Write two details about solids.

_____

_____

Tell what happens
to the shape of a toy
when you pick it up.

78

The properties of a solid can change. A solid can change shape if you do something to it. You can cut a solid to change its shape. You can tear it or fold it. You can bend it or break it. The rope bends. It has a new shape.

Underline how you can change the shape of a solid.

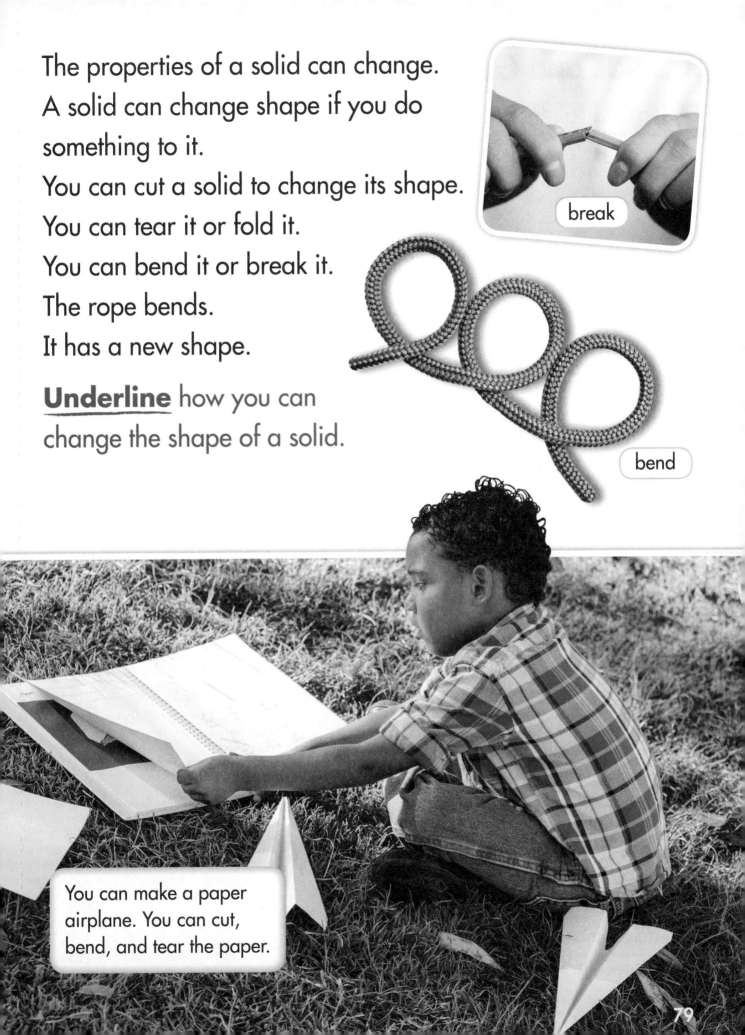

break

bend

You can make a paper airplane. You can cut, bend, and tear the paper.

Liquids and Gases

A **liquid** takes the shape of its container.

You can pour a liquid.

Water is a liquid.

A **gas** can change shape and size.

A gas takes the shape of its container.

A gas fills all of its container.

You cannot see most gases.

Air is a gas.

(Circle) something that contains a liquid. **Tell** one thing about each kind of matter.

Quick Lab

Water Changes
Fill two cups with water. Place one by a window. Place the other in the shade. Check them in three days. How did the water change? **TEKS 5B**

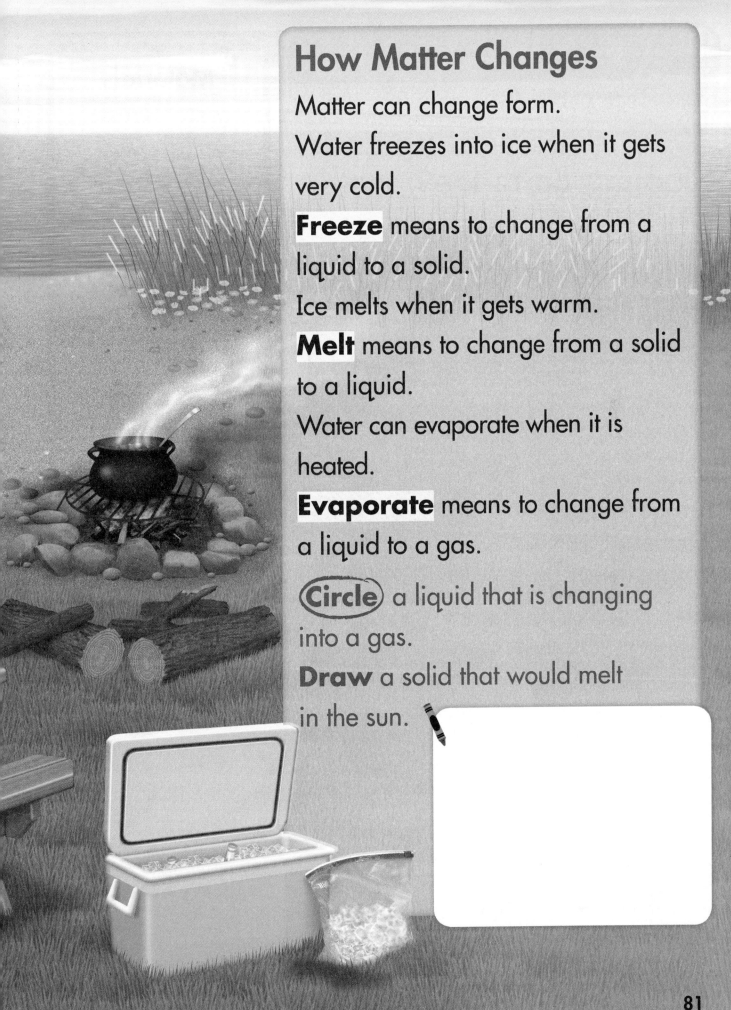

How Matter Changes

Matter can change form.

Water freezes into ice when it gets very cold.

Freeze means to change from a liquid to a solid.

Ice melts when it gets warm.

Melt means to change from a solid to a liquid.

Water can evaporate when it is heated.

Evaporate means to change from a liquid to a gas.

(Circle) a liquid that is changing into a gas.

Draw a solid that would melt in the sun.

What does heating and cooling do to ice?

Follow a Procedure

☐ **1.** Put one bag of ice in the bowl of warm water.

☐ **2.** Put the other bag of ice in the bowl of cold water.

warm water

cold water

Materials

2 bags of ice

bowl of cold water

bowl of warm water

timer

Inquiry Skill
You **record** and **organize data** when you add your observations to a chart.

☐ **3. Predict** Look at each bag. **Record** what you think will happen to the ice.

☐ **4.** Wait five minutes.
   Look at the bags of ice again.
   Record how the ice cubes changed.

	Warm Water	Cold Water
Predict		
What Happens		

Analyze and Conclude

5. Interpret Data   How did the ice change in
   the cold water?

_____

_____

   How did the ice change in the warm water?

- -

_____

6. Infer   Why did the bags of ice change in
   different ways?

_____

- -

_____

_____

Frozen Waterfalls

TEKS 5B

Have you seen waterfalls? They are fun to watch. Some waterfalls freeze in cold temperatures. The waterfalls at Turnagain Arm, Alaska, can freeze in winter. The falls are solid ice! They do not flow. They do not change shape.

Some people like to climb the falls when the falls freeze. It is very dangerous. Only skilled people can do it.

The frozen waterfalls along Turnagain Arm are south of Anchorage, Alaska.

Predict what would happen to the falls if the temperature got warmer.

Identify how the falls would change if the temperature got warmer.

Vocabulary Smart Cards

- evaporate
- freeze
- gas
- liquid
- mass
- matter
- melt
- solid
- weight

Play a Game!

Cut out the cards.

Work with a partner. Cover up the words on each card.

Look at the picture and guess the word.

solid

sólido

matter

materia

liquid

líquido

mass

masa

gas

gas

weight

peso

anything that takes up space

cualquier cosa que ocupa espacio

matter that has its own shape and size

materia que tiene forma y tamaño propios

the amount of matter in an object

cantidad de materia de un objeto

matter that takes the shape of its container

materia que toma la forma del recipiente que la contiene

how heavy an object is

cuán pesado es un objeto

matter that can change size and shape

materia que puede cambiar de tamaño y forma

 86

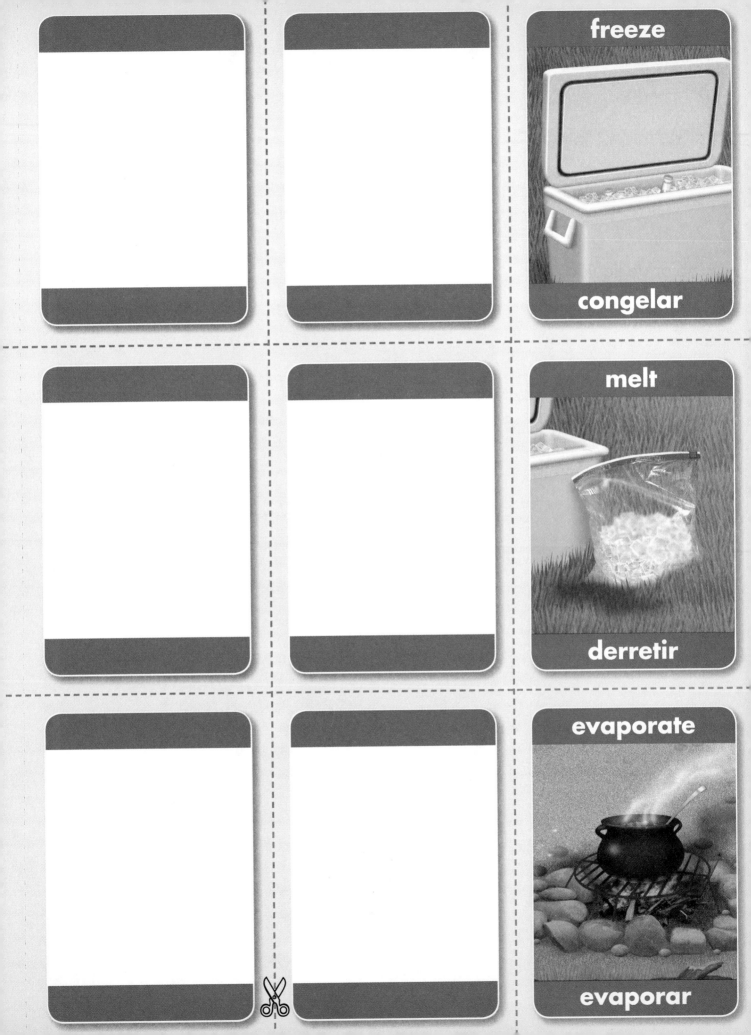

freeze

congelar

melt

derretir

evaporate

evaporar

to change from a
liquid to a solid

cambiar de líquido
a sólido

to change from a
solid to a liquid

cambiar de sólido
a líquido

to change from a
liquid to a gas

cambiar de líquido a
gas

Lesson 1   TEKS 5A

1. What takes up space? **Circle** the letter.

A force

C matter

B speed

D direction

2. Classify How can you group the blocks in the picture?

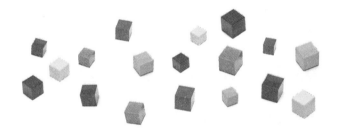

3. Classify Circle the object that does not belong.
Draw an ✗ on the smallest object.

4. Classify Look at the clock.
Draw something that has the same shape.

Lesson 2 ⬥ TEKS 5B

5. Describe Write what a gas can do.

_____

6. Apply Draw three ways that water can change.

freeze	melt	evaporate

TEKS Practice

7. Tell how water changes from a liquid to a gas.

Chapter 2

Lesson 1   What is matter?

TEKS: 5A

Lesson 2   What are solids, liquids, and gases?

TEKS: 5A, 5B

★ TEKS Practice: Chapter Review

Read each question and circle the best answer.

1 Kristen wants to sort the leaves into two groups.

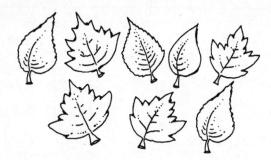

How can she sort them?

A By color

B By weight

C By shape

D All of the above

2 Gabe left his dog's water bowl outside all night. The bowl was filled with ice in the morning. What might have happened?

F Cold air made the water turn into a gas.

G Cold air made the water freeze.

H Warm air made the water melt.

J Warm air made the water evaporate.

3 How long is the longest leaf?

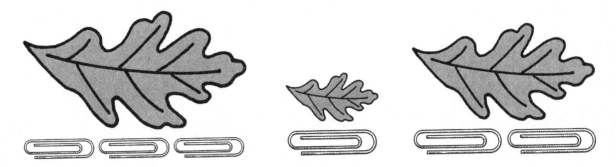

   A One paper clip long

   B Two paper clips long

   C Three paper clips long

   D Four paper clips long

---

4 Sofia observes a snail for five minutes. What tool should she use to measure how far the snail moves?

   F Ruler

   G Pan balance

   H Thermometer

   J Hand lens

If you have trouble with . . .				
Question	1	2	3	4
See chapter (lesson)	2 (1)	2 (2)	1 (3)	1 (3)
TEKS	5A	5B	5A	2C

What makes food cook on a grill?

Energy

Lesson 1 How do we use energy?

Lesson 2 What gives off heat?

Lesson 3 What is light?

Lesson 4 What is sound?

FOCUS ON TEKS

What can energy do?

6A

Tell what you know about the coals in the grill.

🔺 **Texas Essential Knowledge and Skills**

TEKS 6A Identify and discuss how different forms of energy such as light, heat, and sound are important to everyday life. **8D** Demonstrate that air is all around us and observe that wind is moving air.
Process TEKS: 1A, 1B, 2A, 2B, 2C, 2D, 2E, 4A

What does light do?

☑ **1.** Turn on the flashlight.

☑ **2.** Shine it at the plastic wrap.

Observe.
Is the light bright?
Is the light dim?
Is there no light?

☑ **3.** Repeat with
other materials. **Record.**

Materials
flashlight

cardboard

white paper

plastic wrap

foil   wax paper

Inquiry Skill
After you **observe**, you can collect data.

Material	Bright Light	Dim Light	No Light

Explain Your Results

4. Observe What did the light do?

_____

_____

_____

Focus on Cause and Effect

Connect to **Reading** Read Together

You will practice the reading strategy **cause and effect** in this chapter. A cause is why something happens. An effect is what happens.

A Windy Day

It is a windy day.
You run across the park.
You hold your kite high.
The wind catches it.
Soon the kite flies in the sky!

Practice It!

Write what happens when the wind catches a kite.

Cause

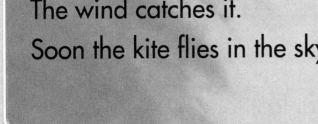
The wind catches the kite.

Effect

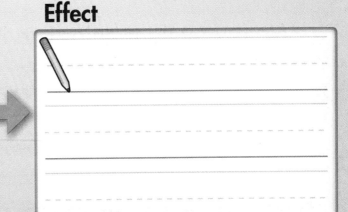

How do we use energy?

I will know TEKS 6A
I will know how energy is used. (Also 2B, 2E)

Vocabulary
electricity
energy

Connect to
Social Studies

Social Studies TEKS 2B, 16A

The first electric lights did not last long. They would burn out quickly. Thomas Edison and his team worked hard. They found a material that would not burn out quickly.

Write why light bulbs are important.

 **Quick Lab**

TEKS 6A, 2B, 2E

What kind of energy can you see and feel?

Materials

flashlight

☐ **1.** Keep the flashlight off. Hold your hand in front of it. **Observe** how it feels.

☐ **2.** Take your hand away. Turn the flashlight on. **Record** what you see.

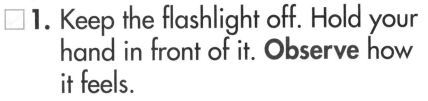

_____

☐ **3.** Hold your hand in front of the flashlight again. **Record** what you feel.

_____

_____

Explain Your Results

4. What change can you feel?   **heat**   **light**

5. What change can you see?   **heat**   **light**

6. Why is light from the flashlight important?

_____

_____

_____

Energy

Click! You turn on the lamp. Electricity makes the lamp glow. The lamp will not glow without electricity.

Electricity is a kind of energy. **Energy** can cause change or do work.

Cause and Effect Tell what happens if you turn off electricity to the lamp.

The lamp uses electricity to glow.

Draw another item that uses electricity that could be in this room.

Electricity makes the fan move the air.

A vacuum uses electricity to clean the carpet.

A laptop uses electricity to turn on and off.

Cars and Energy

Cars use energy.

Most cars get energy from fuel.
Some fuel is burned to make
heat or power.

Cars use gasoline for fuel.
A car's engine burns the gasoline.
The car has energy to move.

Tell how fuel is important in your
everyday life.

Cars get gasoline from
gas pumps.

Quick Lab

Making Things Work
Identify something that
uses energy. What
kind of energy makes
it work? Tell how that
thing is important in
your life. ➤ TEKS 6A

Using Energy

Moving water has energy.
Moving water turns the waterwheel in the picture.

Batteries store energy.
Batteries change the stored energy to electricity.
The toy car uses electricity to move.

Wind the key on the robot.
The robot stores energy as you wind.
Let go of the key.
The robot moves.
The stored energy changes to moving energy.

Discuss where the waterwheel gets energy to move.

Write where each object gets energy.

Texas

Lesson

2

What gives off heat?

I will know TEKS 6A
I will know what gives off heat. (Also **2E**, **4A**)

Vocabulary
heat

Connect to
Math

Math TEKS 2E

Hector lives in Austin, Texas. He looks at a thermometer to check the temperature.
His cousin Claudia lives near El Paso, Texas. She checks the thermometer at her house. Look at the thermometers.

Which city is warmer? Circle it.

Austin, Texas

El Paso, Texas

Lab zone Quick Lab

TEKS 6A, 2E, 4A

How can texture affect the heat produced by rubbing?

Materials

2 plastic squares

2 sandpaper squares

clock with second hand

☐ **1.** Rub 2 plastic squares together for 10 seconds. Feel them. **Record.**

☐ **2.** Repeat using the sandpaper squares. **Record.**

Explain Your Results

3. Which material felt warmer? Explain.

4. Infer   Does rubbing rougher materials together produce more or less heat?

Heat from Sunlight

Heat comes from the sun.
Sunlight warms the land.
Sunlight warms the water.
Sunlight warms the air.

Heat moves from warmer
places to cooler places.
Heat moves from warmer objects
to cooler objects.

Identify and **discuss** how heat
is important to everyday life.

The sand feels warmer
on a sunny day than on
a cloudy day.

Write why you might feel cooler in the shade.

Discuss how a cool beach towel gets warmer in the sun at the beach.

Heat from People

Heat comes from people.
Rub your hands together fast.
How do your hands feel?
Your hands feel warm.
Rubbing your hands together
makes heat.
Running makes heat too.

Cause and Effect How can
you make heat with your
hands?

 **Quick Lab**

Make Heat
Run in place. How do
you feel? How is this
heat energy important
to your life? TEKS 6A

You make heat when
you move.
You can feel the heat
when you run.

Heat from Fire

We use heat in our everyday lives.
Look at the picture below.
Heat comes from the fire.
The heat warms the food.
The heat warms the air.

Draw arrows on the pictures
to identify how heat is moving.
Discuss two other things that can
give off heat.

Heat comes from a
burning candle.

Heat from the stove
makes the water hot.

What is light?

I will know TEKS 6A
I will know what light can do.
(Also **2C**, **2D**, and **2E**)

Vocabulary
shadow

Connect to
Reading

The electricity goes out during a storm. The lights do not work. Tell about other things you could use for light. ELA TEKS 28

PEARSON Texas.com

TEKS 6A, 2C, 2D, 2E

Materials

red paper

How does light change the colors you see?

☐ 1. **Observe** Describe how the paper looks with the classroom lights on. **Record.**

☐ 2. Turn the classroom lights off. **Record** how the paper looks.

Light	Describe
Lights on	
Lights off	

Explain Your Results

3. It is easier to see the color of the paper with the classroom lights **on/off.**

4. What do your results tell about how lights are important to everyday life?

What Makes Light

Light is a kind of energy.
We can see light energy.
Light comes from the sun.
Light comes from other stars.
Light comes from candles.
Light comes from lamps too.

(Circle) where light might come from.

Fireflies make their own light.

We need light to help us see.
You can see objects when light shines on them.
You can see objects that give off light.

Identify and **discuss** why light is important to everyday life.

Identify one more object that makes light.

Light Shines Through

Light passes through a window.
Light passes through thin paper.
Light will not pass through you.
You make a shadow.
A **shadow** forms when
something blocks the light.

Tell why you can see the light in
the lanterns.

Cause and Effect Tell what
happens to a shadow when
the light goes away.

Draw a picture of you
and your shadow.

What Light Can Do

Light moves in a straight line. Light bounces off everything you can see. More light bounces off objects that are smooth and shiny. Light bounces back to you from a mirror.
That is why you can see yourself.

Underline what kinds of objects more light bounces off.

Lab zone Quick Lab

Bouncing Light
Look in a mirror.
What do you see?
Look at a window.
What do you see?
Discuss with a partner why you can see yourself in a mirror but not in a window.

🔺 TEKS 6A

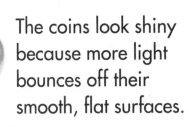

The coins look shiny because more light bounces off their smooth, flat surfaces.

APPLY THE
TEKS
6A

Lights of Dallas

Every city lights up at night. Some cities have buildings with special lights. Dallas, Texas, has some.

Some buildings have light bars on a whole side. There are more than one million lights on some buildings! The lights can show colors and pictures. The lights change too. They can show moving patterns.

Why are lights important? **Talk** about it.

It took weeks to change all the lights on Reunion Tower.

A building in Dallas, Texas, is Reunion Tower. It is a very tall tower. It is 560 feet high. The tower lights up at night. It used to show just yellow colors. People wanted it to look even better. So they changed the lights. Now the tower flashes colors. It shows yellows, reds, greens, and more.

Imagine your own city building. What would it look like at night? **Draw** it.

What is sound?

I will know TEKS 6A
I will know how sounds are
made. (Also **1A**, **2E**, and **4A**)

Vocabulary
vibrate

Connect to
Reading

Think of the different sounds these
instruments make. Put the sounds
together. You might hear some great
music! Now listen carefully. Identify
something you hear. Tell about it. Is it a
soft sound? Is it a loud sound? ELA TEKS 28

Lab zone® Quick Lab

TEKS 1A, 2E, 4A, 6A

How can you make sound?

☐ **1.** Measure 2 meters of string.

☐ **2.** Tie the string tight around a desk.

Put the blocks under the string.

Materials

string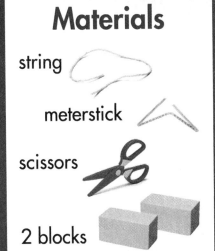

meterstick

scissors

2 blocks

Texas Safety
LAB RULES
Be careful using scissors.

☐ **3.** Pluck the string.

☐ **4.** Tell what happened when you plucked the string.

Explain Your Results

5. **Communicate** How can you change the sound?

Sound

Sound is a kind of energy.

We can hear sound energy.

Sound comes from objects that vibrate.

Vibrate means to move back and forth very fast.

The boy plucks the guitar strings.

You hear sound when the strings vibrate.

Cause and Effect Tell what happens when the boy plucks the guitar strings.

Different guitar strings make different sounds.

120

Sounds Are Everywhere

Sounds are important to everyday life. We use sound to talk to each other. Sounds let you know what is going on around you.

Identify and **discuss** sound. How is sound important to everyday life?

121

Loud and Soft

Listen to the sounds around you.

Some sounds are loud.

Some sounds are soft.

A school bell ringing is loud.

The chirp of a baby bird is soft.

(Circle) the picture below that shows something that makes a loud sound.

Draw an X on what makes a soft sound.

High and Low

Some sounds are high.
Some sounds are low.
You can sing a song in
a high voice.
You can sing a song in
a low voice.

(Circle) the picture that shows
something that makes
a low sound.

Which color heats more?

Follow a Procedure

☐ **1.** Wrap one thermometer in white paper. Wrap the other thermometer in black paper. Use tape.

Inquiry Skill
You **infer** when you use data to answer a question.

☐ **2.** Put the wrapped thermometers in the sun. Wait 1 hour.

☐ **3. Collect Data** Unwrap the thermometers. **Record** the temperatures in the table.

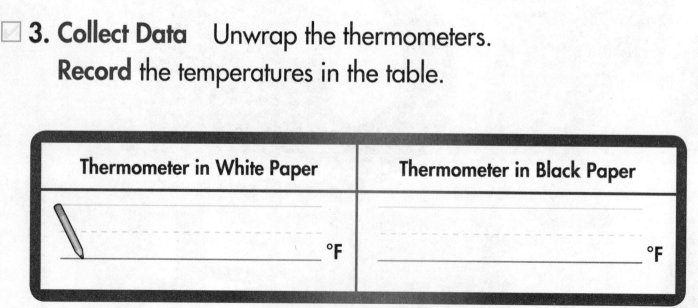

Thermometer in White Paper	Thermometer in Black Paper
_____ °F	_____ °F

4. Repeat. Use black and white fabric to wrap the thermometers.

5. Collect Data Unwrap the thermometers. **Record** the temperatures in the table.

Thermometer in White Fabric	Thermometer in Black Fabric
°F	°F

Analyze and Conclude

6. Which color had a higher temperature? Circle it.

White   **Black**

7. Infer Should you wear dark colors or light colors on a hot day? Why?

Did You Know?

Wind is moving air. We can use the wind to make electricity. Look at the picture. The machines are wind turbines. A wind turbine is like a giant pinwheel. The wind turns the turbine's blades. The turning blades move parts inside the turbine. These parts make electricity.

Texas uses the wind to make electricity. Texas has many wind farms. One wind farm is called Lone Star I Wind Farm. It is near Abilene, Texas. It has 100 turbines!

Could the turbines make electricity if the wind were not blowing? Why?

This wind farm is near White Deer, Texas.

Vocabulary Smart Cards

electricity
energy
heat
shadow
vibrate

Play a Game!

Cut out the cards.

Work with a partner.

Pick a card.

Show your partner the front of the card.

Have your partner make a sentence about the word.

shadow

sombra

electricity

electricidad

vibrate

vibrar

energy

energía

heat

calor (energía térmica)

energy that makes
lamps and other
things work

energía que hace
que las lámparas
y otros objetos
funcionen

dark shape made
when something
blocks light

forma oscura que se
forma cuando algo
bloquea la luz

something that can
cause change or do
work

algo que puede
causar un cambio
o hacer que algo
funcione

to move back and
forth very fast

mover hacia adelante
y hacia atrás muy
rápidamente

moves from warmer
places to cooler
places

se mueve de lugares
más cálidos a lugares
más fríos

 128

TEKS Practice

Lesson 1 🔹 TEKS 6A

1. Vocabulary Draw an X on the object that uses electricity to work.

2. Describe Write about something you use that needs energy to work.

Lesson 2 🔹 TEKS 6A

3. Vocabulary Draw two things that give off heat.

4. Write how heat moves.

TEKS Practice

Lesson 3   TEKS 6A

5. Which object will light pass through?
Circle the letter.

A rock   **C** window

B mirror   **D** apple

6. Explain Write how light is important to your everyday life.

_____

_____

_____

Lesson 4   TEKS 6A

7. Cause and Effect What happens when objects vibrate?

_____

_____

8. Identify something important to you that makes a sound.

_____

_____

TEKS Practice

Lesson 1   How do we use energy?

⬇ TEKS: 6A

Lesson 2   What gives off heat?

⬇ TEKS: 6A

Lesson 3   What is light?

⬇ TEKS: 6A

Lesson 4   What is sound?

⬇ TEKS: 6A

★ TEKS Practice: Chapter Review

Read each question and circle the best answer.

---

1 Grace wants to know if a lamp is giving off heat energy. Which question might she ask to find out?

A Is it making noise?

B Does it feel warm?

C Is it moving?

D Is it bright?

---

2 Fire alarms let people know that there is a fire. They make a loud noise. Fire alarms use sound energy to

F cool off fires.

G pour water on fires.

H blow out a fire.

J tell people to get away from the fire.

3 Diego sees some water on the sidewalk. It is a warm and sunny day.

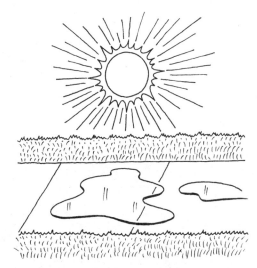

How might the water change by the end of the day?

A It will not change.

B It will run onto the grass.

C It will turn into a gas.

D It will turn into ice.

If you have trouble with . . .			
Question	1	2	3
See chapter (lesson)	3 (2)	3 (4)	2 (2)
TEKS	6A	6A	5B

Why do dogs stick their heads out of car windows?

Movement

FOCUS ON TEKS

6D

How can you describe ways objects move?

Tell what happens when the dog sticks its head out of the window.

 Texas Essential Knowledge and Skills

TEKS 6B Predict and describe how a magnet can be used to push or pull an object. **6C** Describe the change in the location of an object such as closer to, nearer to, and farther from. **6D** Demonstrate and record the ways that objects can move such as in a straight line, zig zag, up and down, back and forth, round and round, and fast and slow.

Process TEKS: 1A, 2A, 2B, 2C, 2D, 2E, 3B, 4A

How does an object on a string move?

Materials

2 erasers

string   meterstick

☑ **1.** Tie one eraser to a long piece of string. Tie the other eraser to a short piece of string.

☑ **2.** Tie the ends of the strings to a meterstick.

☑ **3.** Hold the ends of the meterstick with a partner.

☑ **4.** Pull the erasers up. Let them go. **Observe.**

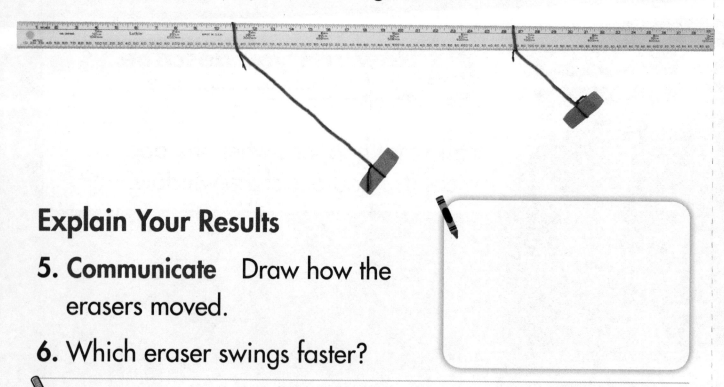

Explain Your Results

5. Communicate Draw how the erasers moved.

6. Which eraser swings faster?

_____

7. Tell other ways the eraser moves.

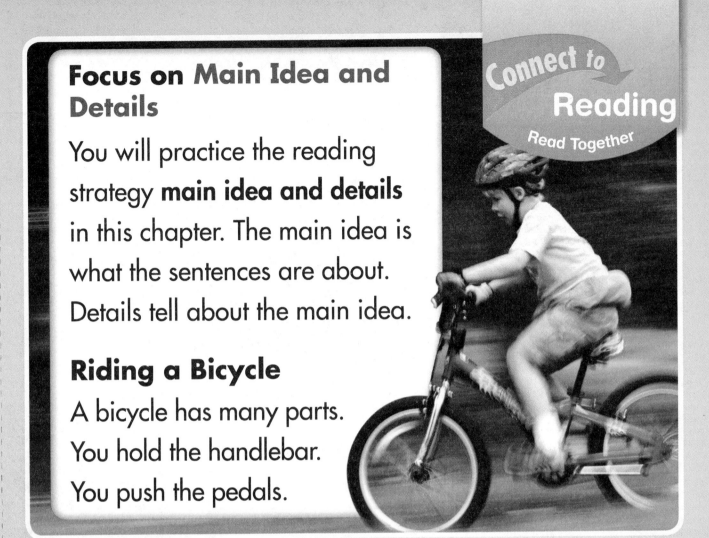

Focus on Main Idea and Details

You will practice the reading strategy **main idea and details** in this chapter. The main idea is what the sentences are about. Details tell about the main idea.

Riding a Bicycle

A bicycle has many parts. You hold the handlebar. You push the pedals.

Practice It!

Write two details that tell about the main idea.

A bicycle has many parts.

Main Idea

Detail

Detail

How can objects move?

I will know TEKS 6D
I will know different ways objects can move. (Also 2E, 4A)

Vocabulary
speed

Connect to
Math

Math TEKS 3D, 8C

Animal	Speed (miles per hour)
squirrel	12
coyote	35
mouse	8

Circle the animal that moves the fastest.

Underline the animal that moves the slowest.

How many miles per hour faster does the squirrel move than the mouse?

_____ − _____ = _____

Quick Lab

TEKS 6D, 2E, 4A

Materials

plastic dropper

plastic cup with water

4 books

tray with waxed paper

How can water move?

☐ **1.** Put one end of a tray on 2 books.

☐ **2.** Put a drop of water on the tray. **Observe** how the drop moves.

☐ **3.** Add 2 more books. Repeat.

Explain Your Results

4. Communicate When did the drop move faster? Explain.

Ways to Move

Objects can move in many ways.

Objects can move in a straight line.

A car can move in a straight line.

Objects can move in a curved line.

The roller coaster moves in a curved line.

Objects can move round and round in a circle.

A Ferris wheel moves round and round.

Draw lines to show how you think the rides at the amusement park move.

Tell how the people on the slide move.

More Ways to Move

Objects can start to move.

Objects can roll.

Objects can slide.

Objects can move back and forth.

Some objects move in a zigzag.

Speed is how quickly or slowly an object moves.

Some objects move fast.

Some objects move slowly.

Objects can stop.

Show a classmate how you can slide.

Show a classmate how you can roll.

Show a classmate how you can move fast.

Label the objects.

fast   roll   slide

On the Move

Work with a partner. Take turns moving. Try the different ways you read about. Record how your partner moved. Record if your partner moved fast or slow. TEKS 6D

Draw a line to show how the people walk across the bridge.

The people walk in a zigzag across the bridge.

APPLY THE
TEKS
6D

Roller Coasters

There are many theme parks in Texas. They each have many rides. Some have more than one roller coaster.

The cars on a roller coaster start close to the ground. Then they go up. They are farther from the ground. Then they go up and down very fast. Then the ride ends. The cars are close to the ground again.

Underline how the cars on a roller coaster move.

Some roller coasters can go 85 miles per hour!

Werner Stengel planned the Shock Wave roller coaster.

Have you ever wondered who thinks up roller coasters?

Werner Stengel is a ride designer. He plans roller coasters. He is very smart.

Werner studies how objects move. He uses math to help plan the rides. He wants to be sure his rides are safe. He wants them to be fun too.

Think of a theme park ride.
Draw it.
Tell how it moves.

What is force?

I will know TEKS 6D
I will know how forces can start, stop, or change the direction of an object. (Also **1A**, **2B**, **2E**, **3B**, and **4A**)

Vocabulary

force

Connect to
Reading

Pull a swing back. Then push it forward. It can go very high! Write about other things you push or pull. ELA TEKS 17B

PEARSON Texas.com

Lab zone Quick Lab

What makes the toy car move?

☐ **1.** Work together. Hold the pencils. Pull back the rubber band.

☐ **2.** Let the rubber band go. **Observe.**

Explain Your Results

3. What made the car move?

Texas Safety
LAB RULES
Wear safety goggles.

4. Predict What will happen if you pull the rubber band back more?

Force

A **force** is a push or a pull.

You use forces every day.

You pull a drawer open.

You push a drawer closed.

Draw an object you pull.

The dogs pull
the dogsled.

Draw an X in the box to show if the picture shows a push or a pull.

Object	Push	Pull

What a Force Can Do

A force can change how objects move.

A force can start an object moving.

A force can stop a moving object.

A force can change the direction of a moving object.

Main Idea and Details **Write** two details about what a force can do.

The children can stop the ball from moving.

More Force, Less Force

Motion is the act of moving.

Use more force.

The motion of an object changes more.

Use less force.

The motion of an object changes less.

Tell how you can change
the motion of a bike more.

Underline how you can change
the motion of an object less.

The children kick the
ball with a lot of force.
The ball moves fast.

Labzone **Quick Lab**

Roll Away
Push a ball hard. See
how far it goes. Push
a ball softly. See how
far it goes. TEKS 6D

How can you describe the location of objects?

I will know TEKS 6C
I will know how to describe the location of objects.

Vocabulary
location

Connect to
Math

🔷 **Math TEKS 7A**

Find two places in the classroom.
Count your steps from your desk to the first place.
Record the number.
Count your steps from your desk to the second place.
Record the number.

Your desk to _____ is _____ steps.
_____(first place)_____

Your desk to _____ is _____ steps.
_____(second place)_____

Circle the place that is farther from your desk.

Underline the place that is closer to your desk.

TEKS 6C

Where are you?

☐ **1.** Look at the town map.

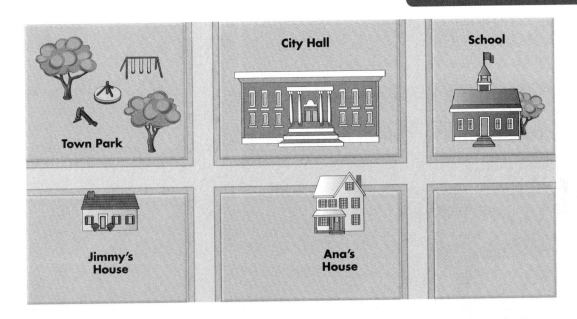

☐ **2.** Put a crayon on Town Park. Circle the house you are closer to.

☐ **3.** Move the crayon to the school. Draw an X on the house that is nearer to the school.

Explain Your Results

4. You are at school. Would it take you longer to walk to Ana's House or to Town Park? Explain.

Location

Location is the place an object is.

An object's location can change.

Motion can change the location of an object.

You use words to tell about the change of an object's location.

Underline the words that tell the location of the butterfly in the picture.

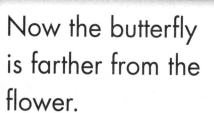

The butterfly is near the flower.

Now the butterfly is farther from the flower.

Quick Lab

Moving Locations
Stand by a wall.
Move to a new place.
What things are now
nearer to you? What
things are now farther
from you? ⬅ TEKS 6C

The butterfly is
closer to the tree.

Changing Locations

Look at the game. Look at the spinner.
The spinner tells how many spaces to move
the game piece.
The game piece's location will change.
This spinner is on 4.
Move the blue piece 4 spaces.

Draw an X on the new location of the blue piece.

Tell how the location of the blue piece changed. Use the words *farther from*.

The spinner is on 2.
Move the red piece two spaces.

Circle the new location of the red piece.

Tell how the location of the red piece changed. Use the words *closer to*.

What is a magnet?

 I will know TEKS 6B I will know that magnets can push or pull some objects. (Also **4A**)

Vocabulary

magnet

attract

repel

Connect to
Reading

How can you hang your drawings on the refrigerator? You can use a magnet! Write about two ways magnets are used in your classroom. **ELA TEKS 17B**

PEARSON Texas.com

TEKS 6B, 4A

What makes the object move?

☐ **1.** Place the paper clip into the cup.

☐ **2.** Touch the magnet to the outside of the cup. Move the magnet up the side. **Observe** the paper clip.

☐ **3.** Repeat with the crayon.

Explain Your Results

4. Communicate Which object moved? Why?

Magnets

A **magnet** is an object that attracts some metals.

Attract means to pull toward.

Main Idea and Details
<u>Underline</u> the main idea about a magnet.

A paper clip is made of steel.

Magnets attract objects
made of iron and steel.
Iron and steel are kinds of metals.
Some buildings are made of steel.

Magnets attract metal.
Paper clips are metal.
Magnets attract paper clips.
Magnets will not attract wood.
Magnets will not attract plastic.
Wood and plastic are not metals.

Circle the objects in the picture
below that a magnet can pull.

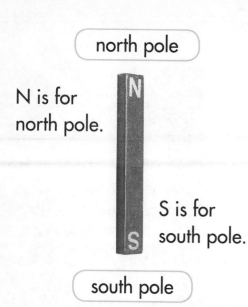

north pole

N is for north pole.

S is for south pole.

south pole

North and South

A magnet has a north pole.

A magnet has a south pole.

Poles that are different attract each other.

Poles that are alike repel each other.

Repel means to push away.

Draw what will happen if you place a paper clip near a magnet.

Quick Lab

Push or Pull

Predict how a magnet can be used to push or pull an object. Now try it. Describe what happens. TEKS 6B

Near and Far

Put a magnet near a paper clip.
The magnet can pull the paper clip
without touching it.
Move the magnet far away.
The magnet cannot pull the paper clip.

Magnets can pull through thin objects
more easily than through thick objects.

Draw an X on the objects the magnets
can easily pull through.

Tell a partner why you
chose these objects.

How can toys move?

Follow a Procedure

☐ **1.** Make the toys move.
   Try different ways.

☐ **2.** Describe how the toys move.
   Collect Data   Fill in the chart.

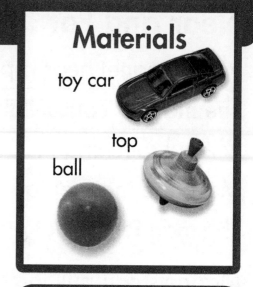

Materials

toy car

top

ball

Inquiry Skill
You **observe** when you gather and record data.

Questions	Answers		
How can I make the toys move?	Car		
	Top		
	Ball		
How can I describe the ways the toys move?	Car		
	Top		
	Ball		

Analyze and Conclude

3. Interpret Data   Which toy moved back and forth?

toy car   top   ball

4. Which toy moved up and down?

toy car   top   ball

5. Which toy moved round and round?

toy car   top   ball

6. Predict   Choose another object. Tell all the ways you think it can move. Explain why.

_____

_____

_____

Did You Know?

 TEKS 6B

Think of the different things magnets can pull. Did you think of cereal? Iron is added to some cereals. Iron is a nutrient. Some cereal flakes have a lot of iron. Crush the cereal flakes. A strong magnet can pull out pieces of cereal with iron.

Write why magnets attract parts of cereal flakes.

Vocabulary Smart Cards

attract
force
location
magnet
repel
speed

Play a Game!

Cut out the cards.

Work with a partner.

Pick a card.

Show your partner the front of the card.

Have your partner tell what the word means.

magnet

imán

speed

rapidez

attract

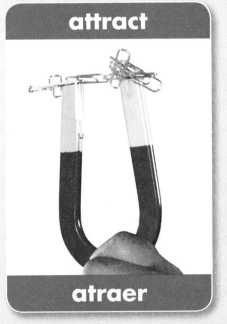

atraer

force

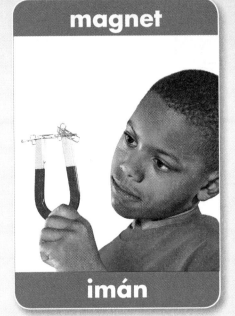

fuerza

repel

repeler

location

ubicación

how quickly or slowly
an object moves

qué tan rápido
o tan lento se
mueve algo

an object that attracts
some metals

objeto que atrae
algunos metales

a push or a pull

empujón o jalón

to pull toward

jalar

the place where
something is

lugar donde está algo

to push away

apartar

TEKS Practice

Lesson 1 TEKS 6D

1. Vocabulary What is speed?

_____

2. Apply Draw a line to show each way of moving.

zigzag	straight	round and round

Lesson 2 TEKS 6D

3. Apply Write one way you use a force.

_____

_____

4. Main Idea and Details
Underline two details below.
The hockey player moves the puck
in many ways. The player hits the
puck hard. The puck moves fast.

TEKS Practice

Lesson 3 🔹 TEKS 6C

5. Which words can describe the change in the location of an object? **Circle** the letter.

   A distance to

   B farther from

   C location

   D greater than

Lesson 4 🔹 TEKS 6B

6. Which object can a magnet pull? **Circle** the letter.

   A rubber eraser

   B metal paper clip

   C wood block

   D plastic toy

7. **Describe** how a magnet is used to push or pull an object.

_____

_____

_____

_____

TEKS Practice

Lesson 1 How can objects move?

TEKS: 6D

Lesson 2 What is force?

TEKS: 6D

Lesson 3 How can you describe the location of objects?

TEKS: 6C

Lesson 4 What is a magnet?

TEKS: 6B

Read each question and circle the best answer.

---

1 José used a magnet to move another magnet.

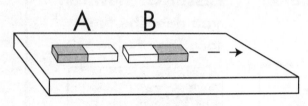 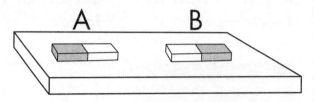

Magnet B moved

A farther from magnet A.

B nearer to magnet A.

C under magnet A.

D over magnet A.

---

2 How does a Ferris wheel move?

F In a zigzag

G Back and forth

H Round and round

J Side to side

3 Josh is making a table of how we use energy.

Ways Energy Is Used

Type of Energy	How We Use It
Light	Lamp to see things
Sound	Voice to talk
Heat	

What should Josh write in the empty space?

A Fire to cook food

B Music to sing to

C Balloons for a party

D Wind to move kites

If you have trouble with . . .			
Question	1	2	3
See chapter (lesson)	4 (3)	4 (1)	3 (2)
TEKS	6C	6D	6A

What affects how far a marble rolls?

Materials

2 metal marbles

6 books

2 metric rulers with grooves

meterstick

Ask a question.

How does ramp height affect how far a marble rolls?

Make a prediction.

1. Will a marble roll farther from a high or low ramp?

(a) high ramp

(b) low ramp

Plan a fair test.

Use two marbles that are the same.

Use two rulers that are the same.

Inquiry Skill
You **control variables** when you change only one thing in your test.

Design your test.

☑ **2.** Draw how you will set up the test.

☑ **3.** Write your steps.

_____

_____

_____

_____

Do your test.

☑ **4.** Follow your steps.

Collect and record data.

☑ **5.** Fill in the chart.

Tell your conclusion.

6. Communicate How does ramp height affect the distance the marble rolled?

_____

_____

_____

Earth Science

177

Where does the soil come from?

Texas

Chapter

5

Earth, Sky, and Weather

FOCUS ON TEKS

7A

What can you tell about Earth, sky, and weather?

Tell about the land in the picture.

 Texas Essential Knowledge and Skills

TEKS 5B Predict and identify changes in materials caused by heating and cooling such as ice melting, water freezing, and water evaporating. **7A** Observe, compare, describe, and sort components of soil by size, texture, and color. **7B** Identify and describe a variety of natural sources of water, including streams, lakes, and oceans. **7C** Gather evidence of how rocks, soil, and water help to make useful products. **8A** Record weather information, including relative temperature, such as hot or cold, clear or cloudy, calm or windy, and rainy or icy. **8B** Observe and record changes in the appearance of objects in the sky such as clouds, the Moon, and stars, including the Sun. **8C** Identify characteristics of the seasons of the year and day and night. **8D** Demonstrate that air is all around us and observe that wind is moving air.
Process TEKS: 1A, 1B, 1C, 2B, 2C, 2D, 2E, 3B, 3C, 4A

Lab® zone Inquiry Warm-Up

Materials

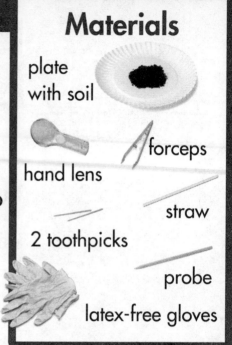

plate with soil

hand lens

forceps

2 toothpicks

straw

probe

latex-free gloves

What makes up soil?

☐ **1. Observe** the soil. Use a hand lens. Describe what you find. How does it feel? What size is it? What color is it?

🔺 **Texas Safety**
LAB RULES

Wear gloves. Wash your hands when finished.

☐ **2. Sort and Compare** Look for differences. Sort the soil into different parts. Put an ✕ by the tools you used.

☐ hand lens   ☐ probe
☐ forceps   ☐ straw
☐ gloves   ☐ 2 toothpicks

Inquiry Skill
You **observe** using one or more of your five senses.

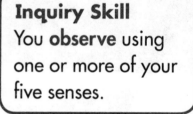

Explain Your Results

3. Which tools worked best?

_____

4. Draw a Conclusion What makes up soil?

_____

_____

_____

Focus on Compare and Contrast

You will practice the reading strategy **compare and contrast** in this chapter. You compare when you tell how things are alike. You contrast when you tell how things are different.

Appalachian Mountains

Mountains

Mountains are very high.
The Rocky Mountains are rough.
The Appalachian Mountains are not.
The Rocky Mountains are higher than the Appalachian Mountains.

Rocky Mountains

Practice It!

Write how the mountains are alike and different.

Compare	Contrast

181

What is on Earth?

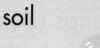

I will know TEKS 7B
I will know that land, water, and living things are on Earth. I will know about streams, lakes, and oceans. (Also **2C**, **2D**, **2E**, and **4A**)

Vocabulary
soil

Connect to
Social Studies

Describe a body of water. *Social Studies TEKS 6A*

TEKS 7B, 2C, 2D, 2E, 4A

Materials

inflatable globe

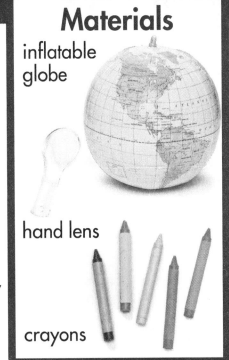

hand lens

crayons

What natural sources of water can you find?

☐ 1. **Observe** the globe. Use a hand lens.

☐ 2. **Record**   Look at the blue shapes. Describe as many as you can. How are they different? How are they alike? Draw a picture of each.

Explain Your Results

3. **Infer**   Which shapes show the ocean? Which show lakes? Which show rivers?

_____

_____

_____

_____

Land, Water, and Air

Earth is made of many things.

Earth has land.

Earth has water.

The surface of Earth has more water than land.

Earth has air all around it.

Color the land green.
Color the water blue.

Earth has natural sources of water. This means that the water comes directly from Earth. Streams, lakes, and oceans are natural sources of water.

Underline natural sources of water.

Kinds of Land

Earth has many different kinds of land.
Plains are large, flat areas of land.
Hills are where the land gets higher.
Mountains are the highest kind of land.
An island is land with water all
around it.

Label the plains, mountains, and island.

Guadalupe Peak is part of the Guadalupe Mountains range. It is the highest natural point in Texas.

Rocks and Soil

Earth's land has rocks and soil.

Rocks are hard.

Rocks can be many colors.

Soil is the top layer of Earth.

Soil can be soft.

rocks and soil

Underline two things that are found on Earth.

Compare and Contrast Tell one way rocks and soil are different.

Water on Earth

Earth has many places with water.

A stream is water that flows across land.

Lakes have land all around them.

The ocean is a large area of salt water.

The ocean covers most of Earth.

Match the word to the picture.

Draw a line.

(stream)   (lake)   (ocean)

Compare and Contrast Tell a partner how a stream, a lake, and the ocean are alike. Tell how they are different.

Quick Lab

What Am I?
Draw pictures of a stream, a lake, and an ocean. Show each picture to a partner. Have him or her identify and describe what is in the picture. Take turns. TEKS 7B

Kinds of Water

The ocean has salt water.

We cannot drink salt water.

We drink fresh water.

Fresh water is not salty.

The water in most streams is not salty.

The water in most lakes is not salty.

We drink water from streams and lakes.

Look at the big picture.
Write what kind of water this would have to be for people to drink it.

189

Fact or Fiction?

Do you think deserts can be cold?

_____

The Chihuahuan Desert is a big desert. It is the largest desert in North America. Part of it is in Texas.

Arizona

New Mexico

Texas

KEY
☐ Chihuahuan Desert

MEXICO

Gulf of Mexico

Parts are in New Mexico and Arizona. Part is in Mexico too.

Deserts can be hot. Many people know that. The Chihuahuan Desert can be 122 degrees Fahrenheit in the day. That is hot!

Deserts can be cold too. The Chihuahuan Desert can be very cold at night. You would need a winter coat! Deserts do not have to be hot. They just have to be dry. That is how scientists identify deserts.

The Chihuahuan Desert is very dry. It can get less than 10 inches of rain in a year. Water can be hard to find! Have a lot of water with you if you visit.

The desert cools after a rainfall. It gets hot again quickly.

Think of a field. It is very hot. It rains a lot. Is it a desert? **Write** why or why not.

What are rocks and soil?

I will know TEKS 7A, 7C
I will know how to describe rocks and soil. I will know how rocks and soil help to make useful things. (Also **1A**, **2C**, **2D**, **2E**, and **4A**)

Vocabulary
humus

Connect to Math

Math TEKS 5B

Maria observed some soil. She found these small rocks. She counted them by 2s. Write to show how she counted them.

PEARSON Texas.com

Quick Lab

TEKS 1A, 2C, 2D, 2E, 4A, 7A

What are soils like?

☐ **1.** Put a spoonful of each soil on a paper plate.

☐ **2. Observe.** Draw. Show colors. Tell how each soil feels.

Texas Safety
L A B R U L E S
Wash your hands when done.

Loam

Sandy Soil

Explain Your Results

3. Communicate   Describe what you see in the soil.

Rocks

Rocks are nonliving things.
Nonliving things do not grow or
change on their own.
Rocks come from Earth.

Write about a place where you can
find rocks.

Enchanted Rock looks
like a dome. It is made
of pink granite. It rises
425 feet above ground.

Rocks can be different sizes.

Rocks can be different shapes.

Rocks can be different colors.

Rocks can feel smooth or rough.

Tell about the rock shown below.

Crystals formed inside this rock.

Parts of Soil

Tiny bits of rock are in soil.
These tiny bits of rock are
different sizes.
Bits of clay are the smallest size.
Bits of silt are bigger than bits of clay.
Bits of sand are the biggest size.

Humus is in soil.
Humus is small pieces of dead
plants and animals.
Air and water are in soil too.

Observe the pictures. Compare them.
How are the parts of soil different?
Describe them to a partner.

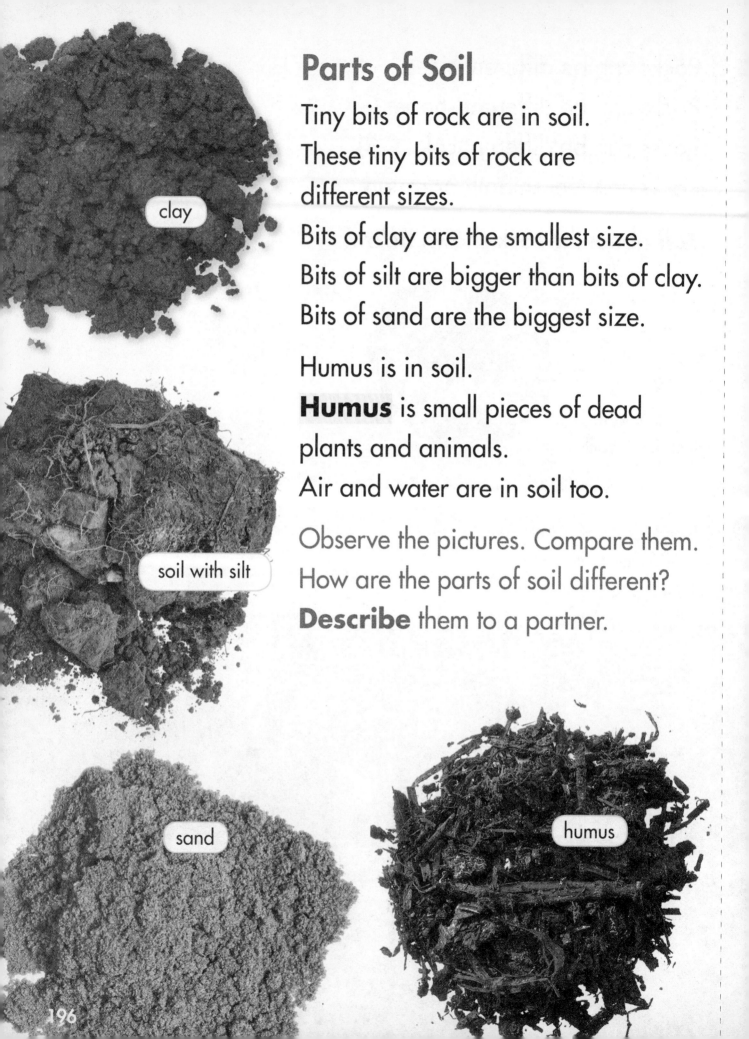

clay

soil with silt

sand

humus

Clay Soil

Soils from different places can have different parts.

Soils can be different colors.

Soils can be smooth or rough.

Clay soil is made mostly of clay.

Clay soil can feel smooth and sticky.

Some clay soil is red.

Clay soil does not have a lot of air.

Many plants do not grow well in clay soil.

Write about the soil in the picture.

This soil is made of clay.

Soil with Silt and Sandy Soil

Some soil is mostly made of silt.
Soil with silt can feel smooth.
Soil with silt is often brown.
Plants often grow well in soil
with silt.

These hills have soil with silt.

Sandy soil is mostly made of sand.
Sandy soil feels dry and rough.
Often sandy soil is tan.
Sandy soil does not hold water well.
Most plants do not grow well
in sandy soil.

Compare and Contrast
Write one way that soil with silt is
different from sandy soil.

_____

_____

This desert has sandy soil.

Loam soil is best for gardens.

loam

Loam

Loam has clay, silt, and sand.

Loam has humus too.

Loam feels wet.

Loam is often dark brown.

Loam has the right amount of water and air.

Plants grow well in loam soil.

Circle what is in loam.

Draw how you could use loam.

199

Ways to Use Soil

People use soil in many ways. They use loam to grow fruits and vegetables. People and animals eat fruits and vegetables.

People use clay to make pots and bowls. We use pots and bowls to hold food.

Sand is put in bags to make sandbags. They can be used to stop water from coming on land. **Underline** the ways people use soil.

Wet clay can be shaped into a bowl or pot. It gets hard when it dries.

Sandbags help prevent a flood.

Sand is used to make glass. Windows are made of glass.

Ways to Use Rocks

People use rocks too.
They use rocks to make buildings.
We live in buildings.

They use rocks to make sidewalks.
We walk on the rock paths.

Look around the room. Look in a magazine. Find something that is made using soil or rock. **Tell** how it is useful.

This house is made of rocks.

This path is made of rocks.

Rocks are used to make chalk.
Kids use chalk to draw on the sidewalk.

How do people use natural resources?

I will know
I will know how to use natural resources. (Also 2D, 3E, and 4A)

Vocabulary
natural resource
reduce
reuse
recycle

Connect to Social Studies

🔸 **Social Studies TEKS 6B**

Where do you think wood comes from? Wood comes from trees. Trees grow on the land. Many trees are cut for wood. Wood is used to make different things.

Draw something you have seen or used that is made of wood.

Quick Lab

TEKS 1C, 2D, 3B, 4A

How much water does a leaky faucet waste?

measuring cup   timer or stopwatch

☐ **1.** Place the measuring cup in the sink. Turn on the faucet so the water drips slowly. Let it drip for 1 minute. Use the timer.

☐ **2. Collect and Record Data** Measure how much water is in the cup. Record for 2 minutes.
Predict how much will drip in 5 minutes. Record.

Amount of Wasted Water	
1 minute	_____ oz
2 minutes	_____ oz
5 minutes	_____ oz

Explain Your Results
3. Why should you fix a leaky faucet?

_____

_____

Natural Resources

People use Earth materials for many things.

A **natural resource** is a useful material found on Earth.

Water is a natural resource.

People and animals drink water. People use water to clean. They use water to make useful things. They use water to make food. They add water to clay to make pottery. They use water to make watercolor paints.

Find pictures of ways water helps make useful things.

Rocks and soil are natural resources.
Plants and animals are natural
resources too.

Circle the natural resources in the picture.

Sunlight and Wood

Sunlight is a natural resource.

People use heat and light from the sun.

Sunlight makes plants grow.

Sunlight cannot be used up.

Wood is a natural resource.

People use wood to build many things.

People burn wood for heat.

People can plant trees to grow more wood.

Wood is used to build houses.

Circle the natural resource that cannot be used up.

Underline how people can get more wood.

Write about something else people make with wood.

_____

_____

_____

Oil and Copper

Oil is a natural resource.

Gasoline is made from oil.

People use energy from gasoline
to power cars.

Oil can be used up.

Copper is a natural resource.

People use copper to make wire.

Copper can be used up.

Suppose all the oil on Earth is used up.

Tell what you think might happen.

Gasoline is a source of energy.

Copper is a metal that comes
from Earth.

Reduce, Reuse, and Recycle

You can use natural resources wisely.
You can reduce what you use.
Reduce means to use less.
You can turn off the lights.

You can reuse things.
Reuse means to use again.
You can wash metal cans
and use them again. You can
use a paper bag again.

Tell one way you can reduce
how much paper you use.

Tell one way you can
reuse a plastic bottle.

Draw one way you
can reuse a metal can.

You can recycle.

Recycle means to make used materials into new things.

You can recycle paper, plastic, and metals.

You can recycle many other things too.

Tell a partner about the materials you and your family recycle. Tell how your family recycles the materials. Ask if you do not know.

Quick Lab

Conservation
How can you use less paper, plastic, or metals? Write your plan. Share your plan with your family. Do your plan. TEKS 1C

Milk jugs are used to make things like the bench below.

MADE OF RECYCLED MATERIALS

What causes day and night?

I will know TEKS 8B, 8C
I will know what causes day and night. I will know about objects in the sky. (Also 1A, 1B, 2C, 2D, and 2E)

Vocabulary
rotation

Connect to
Math

Luke counted 23 stars in the night sky. Marta counted 41 stars. Who counted more stars? Math TEKS 2E

Lab zone **Quick Lab**

🔻 TEKS 8B, 1A, 1B, 2C, 2D, 2E

Materials

crayons

What changes in the daytime sky?

☐ **1. Observe** Look out a window in the morning. Observe the sky. Draw a picture of what you see.

🔻 **Texas Safety**
L A B   R U L E S
Never look directly at the sun! It can harm your eyes.

☐ **2. Observe** Look out the same window in the afternoon. Observe the sky. Draw a picture of what you see.

☐ **3. Communicate** Share your drawings with a partner. Compare them to what your partner saw.

Explain Your Results

4. How are your two drawings of the sky different from each other?

Day Sky

The sun is in the day sky.
The sun makes the day sky bright.
You may see clouds in the day sky.
You may see birds in the day sky.
Sometimes you can see the moon
in the day sky too.

Tell about the day sky in the picture.

The Sun

The sun is a star.

It is bigger than Earth.

The sun is the star closest to Earth.

It looks small because it is far away.

The sun is very hot and bright.

The sun lights the sky even if you cannot see it.

Underline two details about the sun.

Night Sky

The moon and stars are in the night sky.
You may see clouds in the night sky.
You may see birds in the night sky too.

night sky

Circle the things that can be in the night sky.

Moon

The moon moves around Earth.
Light from the sun shines on the moon.
You only see the part of the moon lit
by the sun.
Look at the pictures of the moon.
The moon looks a little different
each night.
The moon looks the same again
about every 29 days.

Draw the different ways the
moon might look.

Changes in the Sky

Observe the sky in the morning, at noon, and at the end of school. Record what you see each time. Show the sun in each picture. Never look directly at the sun.

🔺 **TEKS 8B, 1A**

Sunrise and Sunset

The sun seems to rise each day. The sky becomes light. The sun seems to move across the sky during the day. The sun seems to set at night. The sky becomes dark.

Tell how the sky changes from day to night.

Day and Night

The sun looks like it is moving, but it is not. Earth is moving. Earth spins around and around. One spin around is called a **rotation.** Earth makes one rotation every day.

Earth is always spinning.

It is day when your part of Earth faces toward the sun. It is night when your part of Earth faces away from the sun. The rotation of Earth causes day and night.

Write what causes day and night.

_____

_____

_____

_____

What is the water cycle?

 I will know TEKS 7B, 5B
I will know the water cycle.
I will know how water
changes form. (Also **2D**, **2E**,
3B, and **4A**)

Vocabulary
water vapor

Connect to
Math

Suppose it rained all day
long. Look at the clock.
It shows the time when
the rain stopped. What
time did the rain stop?

🔺 Math TEKS 7E

TEKS 2D, 2E, 4A, 5B

What happens to water in the sun?

Materials

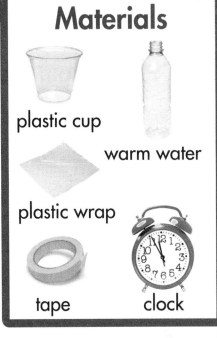

plastic cup

warm water

plastic wrap

tape   clock

☐ **1.** Fill your cup halfway with warm water.

☐ **2.** Tape the plastic wrap over the top of the cup.

☐ **3.** Put the cup in a sunny place for 30 minutes.

☐ **4. Draw** what you see.

Explain Your Results

5. Communicate   What happens to the water?

_____

_____

_____

Water Changes

Drip, drop, rain falls.

Rain comes from clouds in the sky.

Puddles form on the ground.

The sun comes out.

Where does the water go?

Circle where rain comes from.

Tell what happens after the rain stops.

The sun heats the water.
Water in the puddles evaporates.
Evaporate means to change
from a liquid to a gas.

Write what happens last.

First
Puddles form.

Next
The sun comes out.

Last

The Water Cycle

Water moves into the air as a
gas when it evaporates.
Water that is a gas is called
water vapor.
You cannot see water vapor.
Water falls back to Earth from clouds.
This is a pattern. It is called the water cycle.

Water evaporates from the ocean.
Draw an X on another place where
water may evaporate.

Water vapor turns into drops
of water and ice as it cools.
This forms clouds.

The sun heats natural sources
of water. Water evaporates and
becomes water vapor.

Look at the picture.
Follow the steps in the water cycle.

Water vapor turns into drops of water and ice as it cools.
Write what happens next.

Water falls back to Earth as rain, snow, sleet, and hail. These are natural sources of water.

Some water flows into rivers, lakes, and oceans. These are natural sources of water too. The water cycle continues.

How can you measure weather?

I will know TEKS 8A, 8D I will know how to measure weather. (Also 2D, 2E, and 4A)

Vocabulary
weather
temperature

Connect to Math

🔺 **Math TEKS 3F**

Luisa uses a rain gauge to measure rainfall.

Day	Rainfall
Friday	4 cm
Saturday	2 cm
Sunday	3 cm

How much rain fell in the three days?

_____

Circle the day that had the most rain.

Quick Lab

TEKS 2D, 2E, 4A, 8A

Materials

thermometer

When is it warm or cool?

☐ **1.** Put the thermometer outside in the morning.

☐ **2.** What is the temperature? **Record.**

☐ **3.** What is the afternoon temperature?

Explain Your Results

4. When was it cooler? When was it warmer?

5. Infer Why did the temperature change?

Weather

Weather is what it is like outside.
Weather changes from day to day.
Weather may be windy or calm.
Weather may be wet or dry.
Weather may be sunny or cloudy.
Weather may be hot or cold.

What kind of weather would be best
for a picnic?

Different clouds bring different weather.

Look at the pictures.
Write how the clouds might look on a rainy day.

Dark clouds bring rain or snow.

Fluffy white clouds are a sign of fair weather.

Weather Tools

You can use tools to measure weather.
A thermometer measures temperature.
Temperature is how hot or cold
something is.
The numbers show the temperature.
The red line goes up as the air
gets warmer.
The red line goes down as the air
gets cooler.

(Circle) the thermometer that matches
the weather in the picture.

You can measure
temperature in
degrees Fahrenheit
and degrees Celsius.

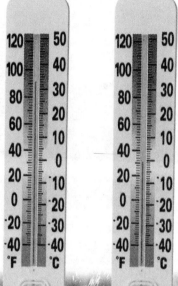

More Weather Tools

A rain gauge measures rain. The numbers tell how much rain has fallen.

A wind sock shows wind direction. Wind is moving air. Air is all around us.

Tell a partner two things about the weather in the picture.

Wind

Wave your hand in front of your face. Feel the wind. Move to different parts of the room. Wave your hand again. What do you feel? Where is the air? ✦ TEKS 8D

Rain falls into the open top of the rain gauge.

The wind blows through a wind sock.

Wet Weather

A thunderstorm has rain, lightning, and thunder.

It can also have hail.

Hail is ice that falls from clouds.

A hurricane is a very bad storm.

The wind blows very hard.

The rain is very heavy.

Rain can turn to sleet in cold weather.

Sleet is frozen rain.

Underline the words above that tell what a thunderstorm has.

 Quick Lab

A Week of Weather
Make a weather chart. Write what the weather is like each day. Tell how the weather changed.

TEKS 8A

There has been snow in many places in Texas, including Odessa, Fort Worth, and Dallas.

Snow is frozen water.
The water freezes high in the air.
Snow falls in very cold weather.
Sometimes snow freezes on the ground. The ground is icy.
A winter storm with blowing snow and wind is called a blizzard.

Draw a house after a snowstorm.

What are the four seasons?

I will know TEKS 8C
I will know what the four seasons are. (Also 2D, 2E)

Vocabulary
season

Social Studies

Fill in the chart. Write one word to tell about the weather around you.

Social Studies TEKS 3C

	Yesterday	Today	Tomorrow
Weather			

TEKS 2D, 2E, 8C

paper

crayons or markers

What is the weather like in different seasons?

☐ **1. Observe** What is the weather like now? What season is it now?

_____

_____

☐ **2.** Draw yourself outside in the season now.

☐ **3.** Draw yourself outside in the three other seasons.

Explain Your Results

4. Communicate How does the weather change from season to season?

_____

_____

_____

_____

Seasons

A **season** is a time of year.
The four seasons are spring,
summer, fall, and winter.

Look out the window.
Tell about the season outside now.

Spring

Spring comes after winter.
Spring is warmer than winter.
Days might be rainy.
Rain helps plants grow.
Many animals have babies
in spring.

Underline what season
comes after winter.

The baby bird is born
in spring.

Summer and Fall

Summer comes after spring.
Summer is warmer than spring.
Summer can be very dry.
Many plants grow in the summer.
Baby animals grow in the summer.

Fall comes after summer.
Fall is cooler than summer.
Some leaves change colors.
Some animals store food for winter.

Point to the summer picture.

Point to the fall picture.

Compare summer and fall where you live.

Write how summer and fall are alike.

The Seasons
Make a chart. Label the four seasons. Write one thing about the season you are in now. Then write about the other seasons where you live. TEKS 8C

Thick fur keeps the rabbit warm in winter.

Winter

Winter comes after fall.
Winter can be the coldest season.
It snows in some places.

Some plants die in winter.
Some animals grow thick fur.
The fur keeps them warm.

Tell how winter where you live is different from the picture.

Lab Investigation

TEKS 7A, 1A, 2B, 2C, 2D, 2E, 4A

How are soils different?

Follow a Procedure

☑ **1. Measure** 50 mL of water.

☑ **2. Investigate** Hold a filter cup with sandy soil over a plastic cup. Pour the water into the soil. Measure the time until water first drips out.

Materials

sandy soil in cup*

clay soil in cup*

loam soil in cup*

(*prepared by teacher)

water

timer

3 plastic cups

graduated cylinder

Inquiry Skill
Scientists make careful observations when they carry out an investigation.

Texas Safety
LAB RULES
Wash your hands when finished!

sandy soil

☐ **3.** Repeat Steps 1 and 2 with clay soil and loam soil.

☐ **4.** Record.

Water Drip Times		
Soil	**How much water?** (mL)	**Time when water first drips** (seconds)
Sandy soil		
Clay soil		
Loam soil		

Analyze and Conclude

5. Interpret Data   Which soil let water through fastest?

_____

_____

_____

6. Which soil do you think would help a plant grow the best? Why?

_____

_____

_____

Palo Duro Canyon State Park

Palo Duro Canyon is near Amarillo, Texas. It has many interesting rocks. Water and wind helped make the rocks the shapes they are now. This took a very long time. The canyon has colorful soil too.

Many people visit the canyon. They camp or hike. They like the different rock shapes. You would like it too!

Look at the pictures.
How is the soil different from soil near your home?
How is it the same?

Talk about it with a partner.

The canyon has rocks of many sizes and colors.

Drink a lot of water when you visit. The canyon is very hot.

Vocabulary Smart Cards

humus

natural
 resource

recycle

reduce

reuse

rotation

season

soil

temperature

water vapor

weather

Play a Game!

Cut out the cards.
Put one set of
cards word side
up. Put another
set of cards word
side down. Match
the word with the
definition.

reduce

reducir

soil

suelo

reuse

reutilizar

humus

humus

recycle

reciclar

natural resource

recurso natural

the top layer of Earth

la capa superior de la Tierra

to use less

usar menos

small bits of dead plants and animals in soil

restos de plantas y animales muertos en el suelo

to use again

volver a usar

a useful material found in nature

material útil que se encuentra en la naturaleza

to make used materials into new materials

convertir materiales usados en materiales nuevos

	temperature	**rotation**
	temperatura	rotación

	season	**water vapor**
	estación	vapor de agua

		weather
		estado del tiempo

one spin around

dar una vuelta sobre
sí mismo

how hot or cold
something is

cuán caliente o frío
está algo

water that is a gas

agua que es gas

a time of year

período del año

what it is like outside

cómo está afuera

TEKS Practice

Lesson 1 🟆 TEKS 7B

1. Exemplify **Draw** two kinds of natural sources of water.

Lesson 2 🟆 TEKS 7A, 7C

2. Summarize **Draw** an X on two parts of soil.

Lesson 3 🟆 TEKS 1C

3. Vocabulary <u>Underline</u> two natural resources.

water   cars   rocks

Lesson 4 🖈 TEKS 8B, 8C

4. Write one sentence that tells about day. **Write** one sentence that tells about night.

_____

_____

_____

Lesson 5 🖈 TEKS 5B, 7B

5. Sequence What happens when water evaporates?

_____

_____

Lesson 6 🖈 TEKS 8A, 8D

6. Describe (Circle) two words that tell about the weather in the picture.

cold   **icy**   **hot**

Lesson 7 🖈 TEKS 8C

7. Describe Write what spring is like where you live.

_____

_____

TEKS Practice

Lesson 1 What is on Earth?

TEKS: 7B

Lesson 2 What are rocks and soil?

TEKS: 7A, 7C

Lesson 3 How do people use natural resources?

TEKS: 1C

Lesson 4 What causes day and night?

TEKS: 8B, 8C

Lesson 5 What is the water cycle?

TEKS: 5B, 7B

Lesson 6 How can you measure weather?

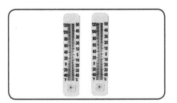

TEKS: 8A, 8D

Lesson 7 What are the four seasons?

TEKS: 8C

★ TEKS Practice: Chapter Review

Read each question and circle the best answer.

---

1 You can use a hand lens to tell

   A how deep soil is.

   B how much sand soil has in it.

   C how much soil weighs.

   D how warm or cold soil is.

---

2 Lea looks at the night sky. She sees many objects. What object will she **NOT** see?

   F The moon

   G A cloud

   H A star

   J The sun

---

3 In what season does the weather start to get warmer?

   A Spring

   B Summer

   C Fall

   D Winter

4 Which object moves in a nearly straight line?

F A falling eraser

G A snake

H A merry-go-round

J A kite

---

5 Mateo and Bella are playing in the snow. Bella throws a snowball at Mateo. How will the snowball move?

A Behind Bella

B Nearer to Bella

C Closer to Mateo

D Farther from Mateo

If you have trouble with . . .					
Question	1	2	3	4	5
See chapter (lesson)	5 (2)	5 (4)	5 (7)	4 (1)	4 (3)
TEKS	7A	8B	8C	6D	6C

Open-Ended Inquiry

🔻 TEKS 8D, 1A, 1B, 2C, 2D, 2E, 4A

How can you see the wind blow?

Materials

newspaper

scissors

1 craft stick

fan

tape

Inquiry Skill
You can use a model to help you **infer.**

Ask a question.

How does a flag show wind blowing?

Make a prediction.

1. Circle your prediction.

(a) A flag will move if the wind blows.

(b) A flag will move if the wind does not blow.

Plan a fair test.

Do not move the flag during the experiment.

Design your test.

☑ **2.** List your steps.

Collect and record data.

☑ **3.** Draw what you observe.

Effect of wind on a flag	
No wind (fan off)	Wind (fan on)

Draw a conclusion.

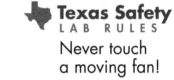

Texas Safety
LAB RULES
Never touch
a moving fan!

4. Communicate How did your flag show there is wind?

5. Was your prediction correct? Tell why or why not.

6. Infer Do you think flags can show the direction of the wind? Explain.

Life
Science

 Texas Essential Knowledge and Skills

Content TEKS
Plants and Animals: 9A, 9B, 9C, 10B, 10C, 10D
Living Things and Their Environments: 9B, 9C, 10A

Process TEKS
1A, 2A, 2B, 2C, 2D, 2E, 3A, 3B, 4A

How is a young orangutan like its mother?

Plants and Animals

Lesson 1 What are nonliving and living things?

Lesson 2 What do living things need?

Lesson 3 What are some parts of plants?

Lesson 4 What are some animal life cycles?

Lesson 5 How are living things like their parents?

Lesson 6 What is a food chain?

 FOCUS ON TEKS 9A

How are living things alike and different?

Tell one way the baby and its mother are alike.

 Texas Essential Knowledge and Skills

TEKS 9A Sort and classify living and nonliving things based upon whether or not they have basic needs and produce offspring. **9B** Analyze and record examples of interdependence found in various situations such as terrariums and aquariums or pet and caregiver. **9C** Gather evidence of interdependence among living organisms such as energy transfer through food chains and animals using plants for shelter. **10B** Identify and compare the parts of plants. **10C** Compare ways that young animals resemble their parents. **10D** Observe and record life cycles of animals such as a chicken, frog, or fish.
Process TEKS: 1A, 2A, 2B, 2C, 2D, 2E, 3A, 3B, 4A

How are flowers alike and different?

Materials

hand lens

paper

different flowers

☐ **1.** Take a flower apart.

☐ **2. Classify** Group the parts that are alike.

Inquiry Skill

Classify means to sort things into groups that are alike and different.

☐ **3. Observe** Compare the parts that are different.

Explain Your Results

4. Communicate How are the parts alike?

_____

_____

5. How are the parts different?

_____

_____

_____

_____

Focus on Compare and Contrast

You will practice the reading strategy **compare and contrast** in this chapter. You compare when you tell how things are alike. You contrast when you tell how things are different.

grizzly bear

Two Kinds of Bears

Grizzly bears live in North America.

Pandas live in Asia.

Both bears have fur.

One bear has brown fur.

The other bear has black and white fur.

panda

Practice It!

Write how the grizzly bear and panda are alike and different.

Compare	Contrast

What are nonliving and living things?

 I will know TEKS 9A
I will know the difference between nonliving and living things. (Also **1A**, **2D**, **2E**, and **4A**)

Vocabulary
nonliving
living

Connect to Math

S T E M

Marco made a bird feeder. He put it in his yard. He observes the bird feeder at the same time every day. He counts how many birds he sees. He made the graph below. Math TEKS 8C

Birds in the Bird Feeder

	Monday	Tuesday	Wednesday	Thursday	Friday
6					
5					
4					
3					
2					
1					
0					

1. Circle the day that Marco saw the most birds.
2. Draw an X on the days that Marco saw the same number of birds.

TEKS 9A, 1A, 2D, 2E, 4A

Materials

plastic
bowl with
gravel

bean seeds

plastic cup
with water

Which is a living thing?

☐ **1.** Put the seeds on the gravel. Barely cover the gravel with water.

☐ **2. Record** your observations.

 Texas Safety
LAB RULES
Never eat or drink anything while doing activities.

Daily Observations

Day 1	
Day 2	
Day 3	
Day 4	

Explain Your Results

3. Infer Which is living? Explain.

_____

_____

_____

Nonliving Things

Nonliving things do not grow.

Nonliving things do not change on their own.

Nonliving things do not have young.

Nonliving things do not move on their own.

Look at the toy box.

Tell why the toys are nonliving.

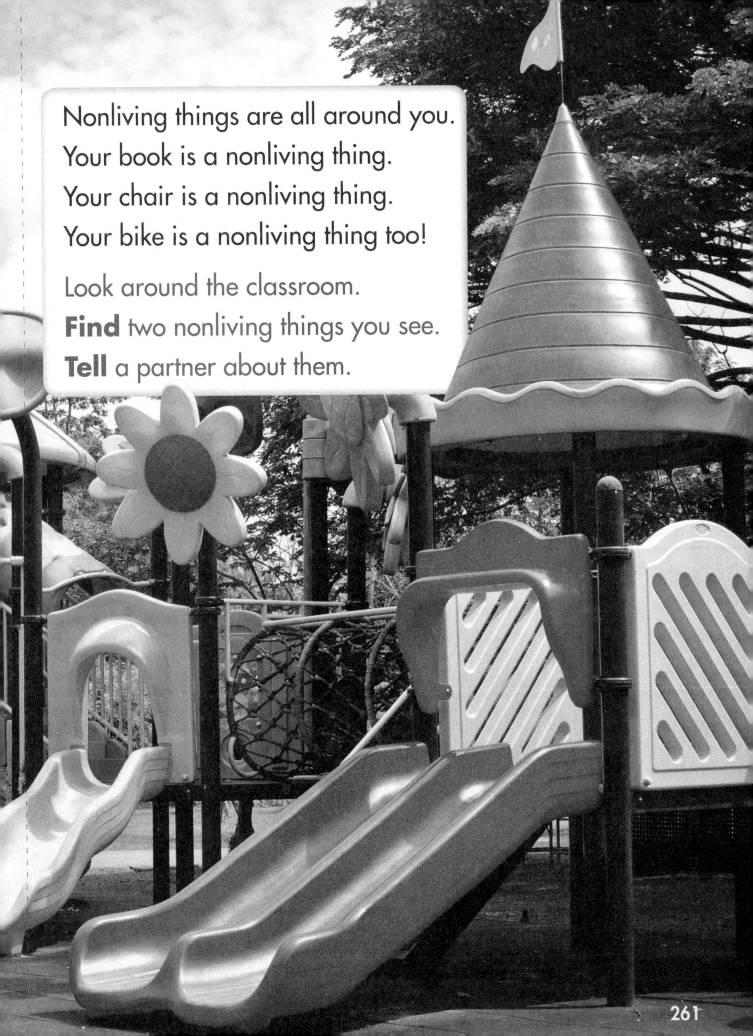

Nonliving things are all around you.
Your book is a nonliving thing.
Your chair is a nonliving thing.
Your bike is a nonliving thing too!

Look around the classroom.
Find two nonliving things you see.
Tell a partner about them.

Living Things

Living things can grow.

Living things can change on their own.

Living things can have young.

Many living things move on their own.

Plants are living things.

Animals are living things.

You are a living thing too.

Look at the picture.

(Circle) two living things.

Draw an X on two nonliving things.

Tell how you know which things are living.

Living and Nonliving

Go outside with an adult. List 10 things you see. Classify and sort the things into living and nonliving. Make a chart. Share your chart with the class. Tell how you know whether each thing is living or nonliving. TEKS 9A

What do living things need?

 I will know TEKS 9A, 9B, 9C I will know what living things need. I will know how living things depend on each other. (Also **2D**, **2E**, and **3A**)

Vocabulary
need
nutrients
shelter

Connect to
Math

Math TEKS 5B

Could you recognize a monarch butterfly? It's easy! They are black, orange, and white.

You can see the butterflies in Texas in the spring.

Gina observes her garden in the spring. She counts the butterflies she sees. How many does she count?

PEARSON Texas.com

TEKS 2D, 2E, 9A

Materials

plant   water

Do plants need water?

☐ **1. Observe** the plant. Add water.

☐ **2. Predict** what will happen.

☐ **3.** Wait 1 day. **Record** your observation.

Explain Your Results

4. Predict   What will happen if you do not water the plant anymore?

Needs

All living things have needs.
A **need** is something a living
thing must have to live.
Nonliving things do not have needs.

Tell about the needs of the bluebonnets
in the picture.

Plants and animals are living things. Plants and animals have needs. People have needs too.

Draw one living thing and one nonliving thing that might be in the picture.

Tell why the things you drew are living or nonliving.

Living Thing

Nonliving Thing

Needs of Plants

Plants need air.

Plants need water.

Plants need light to make food.

Plants need space to live and grow.

Tell how you know the strawberry plants get what they need.

Draw one thing the strawberry plants need.

strawberry plants

Nutrients

Plants need nutrients.

Nutrients are materials
that living things need.

Plants can get nutrients from the soil.

Point to where the strawberry
plants get nutrients. **Write** why the
strawberry plants need nutrients.

Needs of Animals

Animals need air and water.

Animals need food.

Animals get nutrients from food.

Animals need space to live.

Some animals need shelter.

Shelter is a safe place.

Write how the needs of plants and animals are different.

owl shelter

Some animals use trees for shelter.
The owl uses a tree for shelter.
Some animals make their own shelter.

Beavers build
their own shelter.

Look at the big picture. What does
the beaver use to make its shelter?
Circle the words.

rocks   sticks   mud

Needs of Pets

Pets have needs too.

Pets need air and water.

Pets need food.

Pets need shelter and space to live.

Pets depend on people to get what they need.

Tell the ways a pet needs its owner.

People walk their pet dogs. They give their dogs shelter and food.

 Quick Lab

Classroom Pet
Suppose your classroom has a pet rabbit. The rabbit needs a new home. How could you solve this problem? How could you help find a new home for the rabbit? Share your ideas with a partner.

TEKS 3A

Terrariums

A terrarium is a glass tank where plants and small animals live.

You can make a terrarium. You must choose plants and animals that can live together. They will depend on each other.

You can observe a terrarium with a hand lens.

You can record what you observe in a notebook.

Analyze how plants and small animals depend on each other in a terrarium.

The Texas Zoo

Long ago there was no zoo in Victoria, Texas. A man gave a lion to the mayor in 1957. The mayor said the town should have a zoo. The lion could live there.

Years passed. The zoo got more animals. Soon the zoo had 200 animals!

grey fox

People knew the animals needed more space. They built large spaces. They filled the spaces with rocks, soil, and water. They called the zoo The Texas Zoo. Many people still visit the zoo today.

Circle two living things.
Underline two nonliving things.

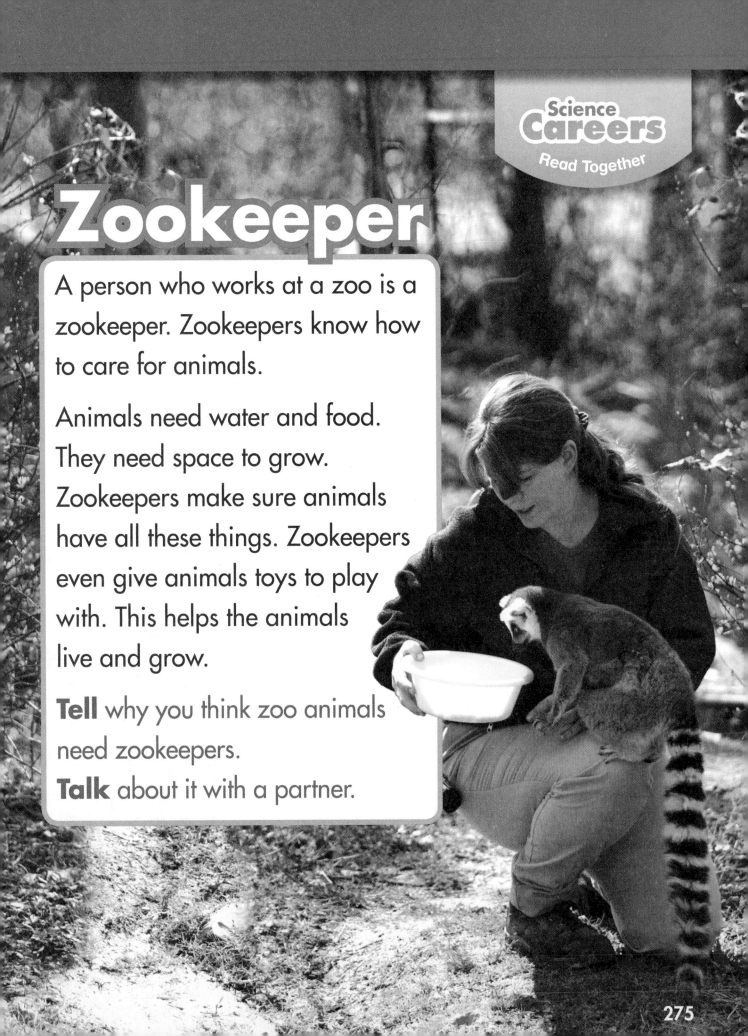

Zookeeper

A person who works at a zoo is a zookeeper. Zookeepers know how to care for animals.

Animals need water and food. They need space to grow. Zookeepers make sure animals have all these things. Zookeepers even give animals toys to play with. This helps the animals live and grow.

Tell why you think zoo animals need zookeepers.

Talk about it with a partner.

What are some parts of plants?

I will know TEKS 10B
I will know the parts of plants.
(Also **4A**)

Vocabulary
root
leaf
stem

 Connect to Math

Math TEKS 2C

Did you know cotton comes from cotton plants? Cotton is a kind of material. Part of the cotton plant is used to make cotton.

Texas grows more cotton than any other state!

Sumi has 36 cotton seeds. Which answer shows another way to write 36? Circle it.

60 + 3   30 + 60
30 + 6   3 + 6

Quick Lab

How do leaves compare?

Materials

hand lens

crayons

Follow a procedure

☐ 1. Go outside. Find a plant.

☐ 2. Look closely at a leaf from the plant. Use a hand lens. What do you see?

☐ 3. **Record** Draw the leaf.

☐ 4. Find a different plant. Look closely at a leaf. Use a hand lens. What do you see?

☐ 5. **Record** Draw the second leaf.

Explain Your Results

6. **Communicate** How are the leaves alike? How are they different?

Parts of Plants

Plants have different parts.
The parts help the plant live and grow.
The parts help the plant get what
it needs.

Underline how the parts help the plants.

Plants Look Different

An iris and a tulip are plants.

They have the same parts.

They do not look alike.

Compare and Contrast Write how
the iris and the tulip are alike and different.

iris

Compare	**Contrast**

279

Roots, Stems, and Leaves

Many plants have roots.

Roots hold the plant in the ground.

Roots take in water.

Many plants have leaves and stems too.

The **stem** takes water from the roots
to other parts of the plant.

The **leaf** makes food for the plant.

Compare and **contrast** the
stem and the roots of a plant.

Draw an arrow to show how
water will move inside the plant.

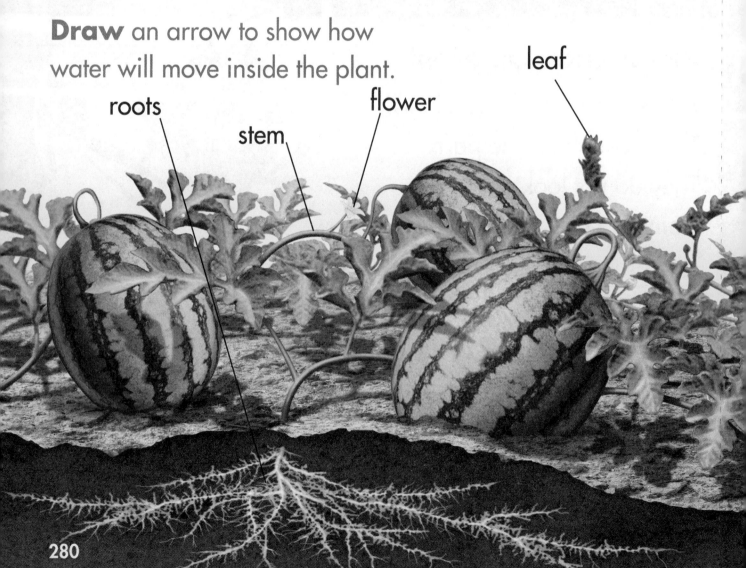

roots

stem

flower

leaf

Flowers and Fruit

Many plants have flowers.
Seeds come from flowers.
Fruits come from flowers too.
Fruits have seeds.

Circle the part of the rose plant where seeds come from.

Identify the plant parts.

Draw a line from the word to the plant part on the rose.

roots   stem   flowers   leaves

Lab zone Quick Lab

Grow a Plant
Get a cup of dirt. Put seeds in it. Put it in a warm, sunny area. Water the seeds. Tell what parts of your plant are growing. Measure with paperclips. Compare with others. 🔻 TEKS 10B

What are some animal life cycles?

I will know TEKS 10D, 10C I will know about life cycles of different animals. (Also **2A**, **2B**, **2D**, **2E**, **3B**, and **4A**)

Vocabulary
life cycle
tadpole

Connect to Math

Liza is a lizard. She is 1 inch long when she is a baby. She grows to be 5 inches long. How many inches did she grow? Math TEKS 3B

1 inch + _____ inches = 5 inches

TEKS 2A, 2B, 2D, 2E, 3B, 4A, 10C

Materials

crayons

computer

How do animals change?

☐ **1.** Think of a baby animal. Use a computer to find a picture of it.

☐ **2.** Use a computer to find a picture of its parent.

☐ **3.** Draw a picture of the baby animal.

☐ **4.** Draw a picture of the baby animal's parent.

Baby	Parent

Explain Your Results

5. Draw Conclusions How are the adult and baby alike? How are they different?

_____

_____

_____

_____

Chicken Life Cycle

Living things grow and change.

A **life cycle** is the way a living thing grows and changes.

A chicken is an animal.

Chickens go through a life cycle.

The chicken begins as an egg.

The egg will hatch.

Hatch means to come out of an egg.

Observe the pictures. **Write** numbers to show the order of the chicken life cycle.

egg

chick

A chick comes out of the egg.

A chick is a young chicken.

The chick grows and changes.

It becomes an adult chicken.

The adult chicken may lay eggs.

The life cycle begins again.

Compare and Contrast Tell how a chick and chicken are alike and different.

chicken

Frog Life Cycle

A frog is an animal.
Frogs go through a life cycle.

Circle the word that names a very young frog.

A frog begins as a small egg.

A **tadpole** will hatch from the egg. A tadpole is a very young frog. A tadpole has a tail and no legs. The tadpole grows and changes. It grows legs. It becomes a young frog.

The young frog grows into an adult. The adult frog does not have a tail. It may lay eggs. The life cycle begins again.

The young frog still grows and changes. Its tail gets smaller. Its legs get stronger.

Observe the life cycle of the frog.
Record the steps in order.

Fish Life Cycle

Fish go through a life cycle too.
Fish begin as small eggs.
Young fish will hatch from the eggs.
The young fish grow into adult fish.
The adult fish may lay eggs.
The life cycle begins again.

Underline the first step of the fish life cycle.

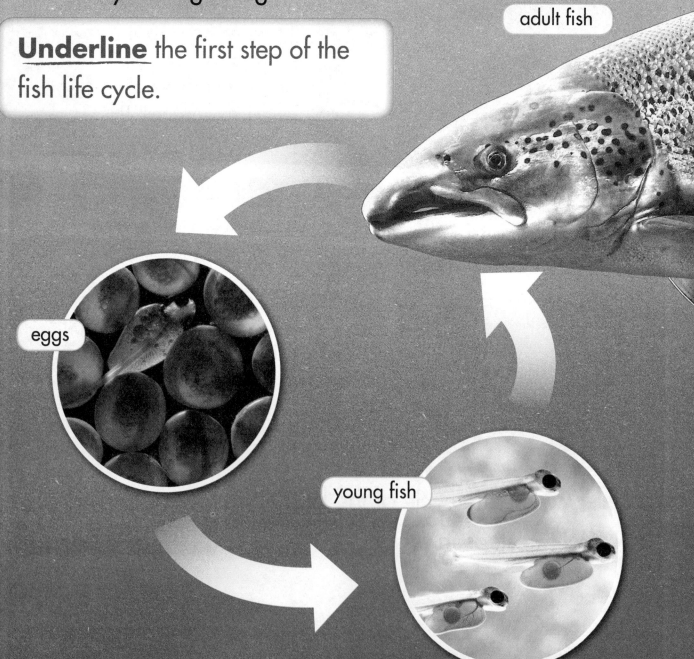

adult fish

eggs

young fish

Record Life Cycles

Draw pictures of the life cycle of a chicken, frog, and fish. Label each step. Record how the cycles are the same. Record how they are different.

► TEKS 10D

Compare and Contrast Tell how a young fish is different from an adult fish.

How are living things like their parents?

 I will know TEKS 10C
I will know that plants and animals look like their parents. (Also **2D, 2E**)

Vocabulary
parent

Connect to
Math

Marta's dog Molly had 7 puppies. Two of them are white. The rest are brown. Circle the number sentence that shows how many brown puppies Molly has.

 Math TEKS 3D

7 – 2 = 5 brown puppies

7 + 2 = 9 brown puppies

Quick Lab

TEKS 10C, 2D, 2E

Materials

baby bingo card

bingo chips

How are babies and parents alike and different?

☐ **1.** Look at the pictures. Talk about what you **observe.**

☐ **2. Classify** Play baby bingo. Match the parent with its baby.

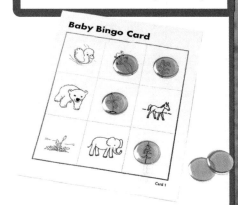

Explain Your Results

3. Communicate Which babies look like their parents?

_____

_____

List the babies that do not look like their parents.

_____

_____

How Plants and Their Parents Are Alike

A **parent** is a living thing that has young.

Plants and their parents are alike.

Plants and their parents can have the same leaf shape.

Draw a line from the young plant to its parent.

young plant

How Plants and Their Parents Are Different

Plants and their parents are different too.
Plants and their parents can have different colored flowers.

Draw a plant and its parent.
Show one way they can be different.

How Animals and Their Parents Are Alike

Young animals are like their parents.

Many animals look like their parents.

Many animals have the same shape as their parents.

Animals and their parents can have the same number of legs.

Underline one way young animals and their parents can be alike.

Draw what the lizard's parent might look like.

The dog and its parent have the same shape.

How Animals and Their Parents Are Different

Young animals and their parents are different too.

Young animals and their parents can be different colors.

Young animals are smaller than their parents.

Compare and Contrast

Write how the chicks are different from their parent.

Quick Lab

Parents and Young
Find a picture of an animal and its young. Glue it to a sheet of paper. Write how the animals are alike and different. TEKS 10C

The cat and its kitten are different colors.

What is a food chain?

 I will know TEKS 9C
I will know how animals depend on plants and other animals. (Also **2E**, **3B**, and **4A**)

Vocabulary
food chain
predator
prey

Jada likes to eat a healthy snack before she plays soccer. The snack gives her energy. Draw a healthy snack that gives you energy.

 ELA TEKS 17A

PEARSON Texas.com

Materials

crayons

What do living things eat?

☐ **1.** Look at the pictures below.

☐ **2.** What does each animal eat?
Draw lines to show your answers.
Then color the plants and animals.

rabbit

frog

eagle

mouse

grass

flies

Explain Your Results

3. Infer What kinds of things do animals eat?

Plants Make Food

Plants need food.

Most plants use water and the sun to make food.

They use air too. The food gives plants the energy they need to live and grow.

Underline the things plants need to make food.

Animals Need Food

Animals need food too.

Animals do not make food.

Animals eat plants or other animals.

Animals get energy from the food they eat.

Circle why animals need food.

Tell what would happen if there were no plants.

The tree makes its own food.

Many owls eat other animals.

Butterflies get food from flowers. The food is called nectar.

Food Chains

A **food chain** shows how energy moves from one living thing to another.

Food chains start with the sun.

Plants use the energy from the sun to make food.

Some animals eat plants to get energy.

Then other animals eat those animals.

Look at the food chain below.

Tell how the fox gets energy from the sun.

Plants make food using the sun.

Predator and Prey

All food chains have predators and prey.

A **predator** is an animal that catches and eats another animal.

Prey is an animal that is caught and eaten.

(Circle) the predator in the food chain.

Draw an X on the prey in the food chain.

A rabbit eats the plants.

A fox eats the rabbit.

Energy and Food Chains

Food chains are everywhere.

Grasslands have food chains.

Deserts have food chains.

Oceans have food chains too.

Draw arrows on the food chain to show how energy moves.

Plants get energy from the sun. They make food.

A grasshopper eats grass. Energy passes from the grass to the grasshopper.

Draw a Food Chain

Work with a partner. Use a computer to gather evidence. Find information about a food chain. Draw a picture of the food chain. Draw arrows to show how energy moves from one living thing to another.

🔺 TEKS 9C, 4A

A frog eats the grasshopper. Energy passes from the grasshopper to the frog.

How can you model a food chain?

Materials

paper plates

crayons or markers

yarn

tape

Follow a Procedure

☐ **1.** Draw the sun on a paper plate.

☐ **2.** Draw a plant on another paper plate.

☐ **3.** Draw a rabbit on another paper plate.

☐ **4.** Draw a fox on the last paper plate.

☐ **5.** Make a model of a food chain. Connect your drawings with tape and yarn.

Inquiry Skill

You can use what you observe to help you **infer**.

☐ **6. Observe** your model. Fill in the chart.

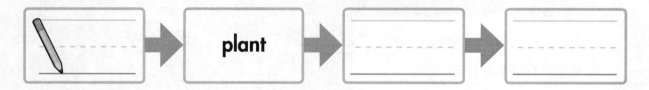

plant

Analyze and Conclude

7. What does a model of a food chain show?

8. Draw where the energy in a food chain comes from.

9. The animals depend on each other for _____.

Did You Know?

The state plant of Texas is the prickly pear cactus. It has stems. The stems are not long. The stems are not thin. They look like green pads. The pads contain water for the cactus.

Tell about a cactus you have seen. Where is it? What does it look like?

Prickly pear cacti can have flowers. Some have yellow flowers. Some have red flowers. Some have purple flowers.

Vocabulary Smart Cards

food chain
leaf
life cycle
living
need
nonliving
nutrients
parent
predator
prey
root
shelter
stem
tadpole

Play a Game!

Cut out the cards. Put one set of cards word side up. Put another set of cards word side down. Match the word with the definition.

nutrients

nutrientes

nonliving

inerte

shelter

refugio

living

vivo

root

raíz

need

necesidad

things that do not grow and change on their own

cosas que no crecen y que no cambian por sí mismas

materials that living things need

sustancias que los seres vivos necesitan

things that can grow and change

seres que pueden crecer y cambiar

a safe place

lugar seguro

something a living thing must have to live

algo que un ser vivo necesita para vivir

the part of a plant that takes in water

la parte de la planta que toma el agua

predator

predador

tadpole

renacuajo

leaf

hoja

prey

presa

parent

padres

stem

tallo

food chain

cadena alimenticia

life cycle

ciclo de vida

the part of a plant that makes food

la parte de la planta que produce el alimento

a very young frog

rana muy joven

an animal that catches and eats another animal

animal que caza y se alimenta de otro animal

the part of a plant that takes water from the roots to the leaves

la parte de una planta que conduce el agua de las raíces a las hojas

a living thing that has young

seres vivos que tienen crías

an animal that is caught and eaten

animal que es cazado y comido

the way a living thing grows and changes

manera en que un ser vivo crece y cambia

how energy passes from one living thing to another

paso de la energía de un ser vivo a otro

Lesson 1 🔻 TEKS 9A

1. Contrast Write one way living and nonliving things are different.

_____

2. Identify (Circle) two living things.

Lesson 2 🔻 TEKS 9A, 9B, 9C

3. What does a plant need to live? **(Circle)** the letter.

A nutrients   **C** toys

B shelter   **D** rocks

Lesson 3 🔻 TEKS 10B

4. Vocabulary Identify and **label** the parts of the plant.

TEKS Practice

Lesson 4 ➡ TEKS 10C, 10D

5. Apply **Label** the life cycle of a chicken.

Lesson 5 ➡ TEKS 10C

6. Compare and Contrast How is a young dog different from its parents?

_____

_____

Lesson 6 ➡ TEKS 9C

7. Vocabulary What is a food chain?

_____

_____

TEKS Practice

Lesson 1 What are living and nonliving things?

TEKS: 9A

Lesson 2 What do living things need?

TEKS: 9A, 9B, 9C

Lesson 3 What are some parts of plants?

TEKS: 10B

Lesson 4 What are some animal life cycles?

TEKS: 10C, 10D

Lesson 5 How are living things like their parents?

TEKS: 10C

Lesson 6 What is a food chain?

TEKS: 9C

★ TEKS Practice: Chapter Review

Read each question and circle the best answer.

---

1 Which of these might a snake use for shelter?

A Air

B Mice

C Rocks

D Sunlight

---

2 What part of a plant takes in water?

F Flowers

G Leaves

H Roots

J Seeds

---

3 A baby bird just hatched. How is it like its parents?

A Both can fly.

B Both have four legs.

C Both are the same size.

D None of the above

4 Ben observed the weather for four days. Then he wrote what he saw in a table.

Weather for Four Days

Day	Sky	How Air Moved	Temperature
Sunday	Clear	Windy	Warm
Monday	Cloudy	Windy	Cold
Tuesday	Clear	Calm	Warm
Wednesday	Clear	Calm	Hot

What tool might Ben have used to measure how the air moved?

F A ruler

G A thermometer

H A rain gauge

J A wind sock

If you have trouble with . . .				
Question	1	2	3	4
See chapter (lesson)	6 (2)	6 (3)	6 (4,5)	5 (6)
TEKS	9C	10B	10C	8A

Where
does a cow get food?

Living Things and Their Environments

Lesson 1 How do plants and animals live in land environments?

Lesson 2 How do plants and animals live in water environments?

FOCUS ON TEKS

9C, 10A

How do animals live in their environments?

Draw an X on one thing a cow needs.

 Texas Essential Knowledge and Skills

TEKS 9B Analyze and record examples of interdependence found in various situations such as terrariums and aquariums or pet and caregiver. **9C** Gather evidence of interdependence among living organisms such as energy transfer through food chains and animals using plants for shelter. **10A** Investigate how the external characteristics of an animal are related to where it lives, how it moves, and what it eats.
Process TEKS: 1A, 2A, 2B, 2C, 2D, 2E, 3B, 4A

How can fur keep animals warm?

Materials

2 thermometers

2 plastic bags

cotton balls

tub with ice water

timer

☑ **1.** Read the thermometers.

☑ **2.** Put one thermometer in each bag. Add cotton balls to one bag.

☑ **3.** Put the bags in ice water for 1 minute. **Predict** what will happen to each thermometer.

☑ **4.** Read the thermometers.

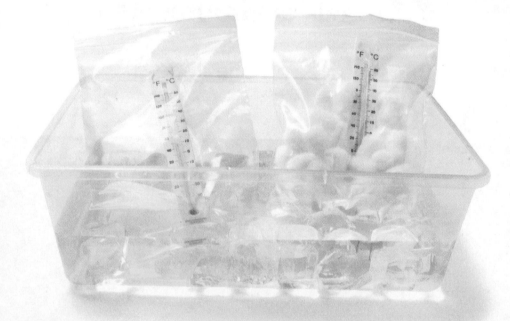

Explain Your Results

5. Tell how the thermometers show that fur can keep an animal warm.

Focus on Main Idea and Details

You will practice the reading strategy **main idea and details** in this chapter. The main idea is what the paragraph is about.

Details tell about the main idea.

Green Tree Frogs

Green tree frogs live near water. Some live in swamps. Some live in marshes.

Practice It!

Write two details about green tree frogs.

Green tree frogs live near water.

Main Idea

Detail   Detail

How do plants and animals live in land environments?

I will know TEKS 10A
I will know how animals and plants live on land. (Also **1A**, **2D**, **4A**, and **9C**)

Vocabulary
desert
environment
forest
prairie

Connect to **Math**

The line below shows how far a snail moved in 10 minutes. Use a ruler. Circle how many centimeters the snail moved. **Math TEKS 7A**

_____

3 centimeters   4 centimeters   5 centimeters

PEARSON Texas.com

320

TEKS 10A, 1A, 2D, 4A

How can you make a model of an animal?

☐ 1. Use a computer to learn facts about your favorite animal.

☐ 2. Draw a picture of the animal.

Materials

computer

clay

paper

pipe cleaners

crayons and markers

☐ 3. Use the craft materials to make a model of your animal.

Explain Your Results

4. Work with a partner. Tell about your animal. Use the model you made. Use your drawing too.

Environments

An **environment** is all living and nonliving things in one place.

An environment has food and water.

An environment has air.

Circle two things you think are in the environment of the raccoon.

food	toys
water	clothes

Land is one kind of environment.
Land has rocks and soil.
Many plants and animals live on land.

Underline the kind of environment
the horses live in.

Draw another animal that lives in a
land environment.

Big leaves help forest plants take in a lot of sunlight.

Forest Environment

A forest is a land environment. A **forest** is land that has many trees and other plants.

Black bears live in some forests. Black bears have sharp claws. Bears use their claws to dig for food. Sharp claws help bears climb trees.

Tell how sharp claws help bears live in forests.

Prairie Environment

A prairie is a land environment.

A **prairie** is flat land that is covered with grasses.

Prairie dogs live in some prairies.

Prairie dogs have sharp teeth.

Sharp teeth help them chew the prairie grass.

Prairie dogs have sharp claws.

Sharp claws help them dig holes in the ground.

They use the holes for shelter.

Underline two things that help prairie dogs live in their environment.

Circle the part of the prairie dog that helps it dig holes for shelter.

Desert Environment

A desert is a land environment.

A **desert** is land that is very dry.

A desert gets very little rain or snow.

Some deserts are very cold.

Plants grow in deserts.

Plants in deserts hold water.

Many animals get the water they need from the plants they eat.

<u>Underline</u> words that tell about deserts.

Tell how getting water from food helps animals live in the desert.

Quick Lab

Local Environments
Go outside with an adult. Look around. Write the plants and animals you see. Write what helps the plants and animals live in their environment.

TEKS 10A

Circle the part of the rabbit that helps keep it cool.

Underline what helps the lizard live in the desert.

This desert is hot during the day. Light-colored skin helps this lizard keep cool.

Heat leaves the body of the rabbit through its big ears.

Rabbits have powerful hind legs to help them hop.

How do plants and animals live in water environments?

I will know TEKS 10A
I will know how animals and plants live in water. (Also 2E, 4A, 9B, and 9C)

Vocabulary
wetland
ocean
aquarium

Connect to

Math

Math TEKS 3B

Ana has an aquarium. She counts 12 fish in all. She moves 5 fish to a new aquarium. Draw an X on the fish Ana puts in the new aquarium. How many fish are left?

TEKS 10A, 2E, 4A

How do some turtles stay warm in winter?

☐ **1. Record** the temperature in each cup. Use the Thermometer Chart.

☐ **2.** Put both cups in a cooler. **Predict.** Which cup will stay warmer?

_____

_____

_____

☐ **3.** Wait 20 minutes. **Record** each temperature.

☐ **4.** Which cup stayed warmer? **(soil/air)**

Explain Your Results

5. Infer where turtles might live in the winter. Explain.

_____

_____

_____

_____

_____

Materials

plastic cup with thermometer

plastic cup with thermometer and soil

cooler (whole class use)

red crayon

Thermometer Chart

Water Environments

Some animals live in water environments.
They get food and shelter there.

Draw an animal that might live in this water environment.

Newts are a kind of animal.
They live part of their lives in water.
They find food and shelter there.

Underline what newts find in a water environment that they need.

newt

Marsh Environment

A **wetland** is an environment
that is covered with water.
Marshes are wetlands.
A marsh has grasses.
Many different kinds of animals
live in marshes.

Blue herons live in marshes.
Herons have long sharp beaks.
They catch fish with their beaks.
Herons have long, thin legs too.

Look at the blue heron.
Draw an X on two parts of the
bird that help it live in a marsh.
Tell how these parts help
the bird.

Swamp Environment

Swamps are wetlands.

A swamp has soft, wet land.

A swamp has many trees.

Alligators live in some swamps.

Alligators are good swimmers.

Alligators use their long, strong tails to help them swim.

Quick Lab

Environments
Make a chart that tells an animal that lives in each water environment. Write what helps those animals live in their environments. TEKS 10A

Write why being a good swimmer would help an alligator live in a swamp.

Draw an X on the part of the alligator that helps it swim.

Ocean Environment

An **ocean** is a large body of salty water.

Some parts of the ocean are deep.

Fish live in the ocean.
Fish have gills.
Gills let fish take in oxygen from the water.
Fish have fins.
Fins help fish swim.

Plants need sunlight to make food.
Ocean plants live where there is light.
The deep ocean is dark.
Plants do not live there.

Main Idea and Details

Underline the sentence that tells how gills help fish live in the ocean.

(Circle) why plants do not live in the deep ocean.

Aquarium Environment

You can observe plants and animals in an aquarium.
An **aquarium** is a water environment in a glass tank or bowl.
An aquarium is an environment made by people.

Tell how people take care of the fish in the aquarium.

aquarium

gills

fins

Stetson Bank

Stetson Bank is a group of coral reefs. Coral reefs are underwater. They look like colorful rocks.

Many people visit Stetson Bank. It is very close to Galveston, Texas. You can take a boat. Then you dive in. Other divers swim with you.

Do you see the fish? It looks like the coral! Reefs are good hiding spots.

Fish love coral reefs. Visitors see a lot of them.

Stingrays swim here too.

You swim down. You see a shark. You see a turtle. You see many fish! They find food there. Some eat tiny plants. Some eat other fish.

Eels eat fish too. Eels hide in the coral reefs. They wait. They jump out. They bite! Sometimes they catch a fish.

Many people in Galveston care for Stetson Bank. They want to protect it from pollution. Do you want to protect it too?

Why do eels live near coral reefs? **Talk** about it with a partner. Think of one way you can help keep the water in Stetson Bank clean. **Draw** a sign to show your idea.

Lab Investigation

TEKS 10A, 2A, 2B, 2E, 3B, 4A

How do birds use their beaks?

Follow a Procedure

☐ **1.** Spread rice on the sponge.

☐ **2.** Float cereal on the water.

☐ **3.** Use the tweezers as one kind of beak. Use the spoon as another kind of beak. Use each tool to pick up a piece of rice. **Record** your observations.

Materials

slotted spoon

tweezers

large, dry sponge

container of water

dry cereal

rice

Inquiry Skill

You **observe** when you gather and record data.

 **Texas Safety**
LAB RULES

Tweezers are sharp! Use them carefully.

Tweezers	Spoon

☐ **4.** Use each tool to pick up some cereal.
Record your observations.

Tweezers	Spoon

Explain Your Results

5. Which tool worked best to pick up the rice? Circle it.

6. Which tool worked best to pick up the cereal? Circle it.

7. Infer   Which kind of beaks are better for getting food from trees or logs?

_____

_____

8. Infer   Why does a bird use its beak to get food?

_____

_____

Did You Know?

Look at the sheep. They are called bighorn sheep. Why do you think they are called that?

Some bighorn sheep live in mountains. Some live in deserts. Some live in parks. Big Bend Ranch State Park in Southwest Texas has them.

The sheep eat yucca plants. They eat wild onions. They eat cactus. A cactus has sharp spines! The sheep scrape off the spines. They use their horns to scrape.

Tell why this is a good idea.

Vocabulary Smart Cards

aquarium
desert
environment
forest
ocean
prairie
wetland

Play a Game!

Cut out the cards.

Work with a partner.

Pick a card.

Say clues about the word.

Have your partner guess the word.

desert

desierto

environment

medio ambiente

wetland

humedal

forest

bosque

ocean

océano

prairie

pradera

all living and
nonliving things in
one place

todos los seres vivos
y objetos inertes que
hay en un lugar

environment that is
very dry

medio ambiente que
es muy seco

environment that has
many trees and other
plants

medio ambiente que
tiene muchos árboles
y otras plantas

environment that is
covered with water

medio ambiente
cubierto de agua

environment that is
covered with grasses

medio ambiente
cubierto de pasto

environment that is
a large body of salty
water

medio ambiente que
es una gran masa de
agua salada

aquarium

acuario

a water environment in a glass tank or bowl

medio ambiente acuático en un recipiente de cristal

TEKS Practice

Lesson 1 TEKS 9C, 10A

1. What helps bears live in forests?
   Circle the letter.

   A gills

   B sharp claws

   C big ears

   D light-colored skin

2. **Write** how sharp teeth help a prairie dog live in its environment.

   _____

   _____

   _____

3. **Classify Draw** two different land environments.

TEKS Practice

Lesson 2 🔺 TEKS 9B, 9C, 10A

4. Vocabulary (Circle) the two wetland environments.

5. Vocabulary Draw an X on the animal that lives in a wetland environment.

6. Draw what you would see in an aquarium.

TEKS Practice

Lesson 1 How do plants and animals live in land environments?

TEKS: 9C, 10A

Lesson 2 How do plants and animals live in water environments?

TEKS: 9B, 9C, 10A

★ TEKS Practice: Chapter Review

Read each question and circle the best answer.

1 How does a rabbit get water in the desert?

   A From animals it eats

   B By staying in the shade so it does not need water

   C From plants it eats

   D By digging deep in the ground

2 What helps a fish move in its environment?

   F Fins

   G Gills

   H Scales

   J Wings

3 An animal has a long, sharp beak and long legs. It uses its beak to catch fish. Where does this animal live?

   A In a desert

   B In a marsh

   C On a prairie

   D In an aquarium

4 What is the correct order in the life cycle of a chicken?

F Adult → Chick → Egg

G Egg → Adult → Chick

H Chick → Egg → Adult

J Egg → Chick → Adult

5 How does Martina know that rocks are nonliving things?

A They are hard.

B They do not move.

C They do not need food or water.

D They can be found in the ground.

If you have trouble with . . .					
Question	1	2	3	4	5
See chapter (lesson)	7 (1)	7 (2)	7 (2)	6 (4)	6 (1)
TEKS	10A	10A	10A	10D	9A

How do parts help a spider survive?

Materials

paper

double-sided clear tape

toothbrush

Inquiry Skill
You can use a model to help you **infer**.

Some spiders make webs. Some web strands are sticky. Prey can stick to these strands. Spiders have hairs on the ends of their legs.

Ask a question.

How do hairs help a spider move in a web?

Make a hypothesis.

1. Circle your hypothesis.

(a) Hair does not help a spider move in a web.

(b) Hair helps a spider move in a web.

Plan a fair test.

Use the same toothbrush to model a spider.

Design your test.

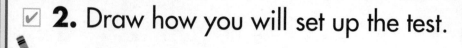

☑ **2.** Draw how you will set up the test.

☑ **3.** List your steps.

Do your test.

☑ **4.** Follow your steps.

Collect and record data.

☑ **5.** Write what you observed.

Smooth Side	
Brush Side	

Tell your conclusion.

6. Infer How do the hairs on a spider help it move in a web? Explain.

Metric and Customary Measurements

Science uses the metric system to measure things.
Metric measurement is used around the world.
Here is how different metric measurements
compare to customary measurements.

1 liter

1 cup

Volume
One liter is greater
than 4 cups.

Fahrenheit

Celsius

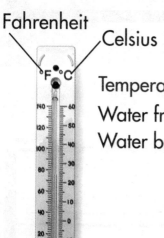

Temperature
Water freezes at 0°C, or 32°F.
Water boils at 100°C, or 212°F.

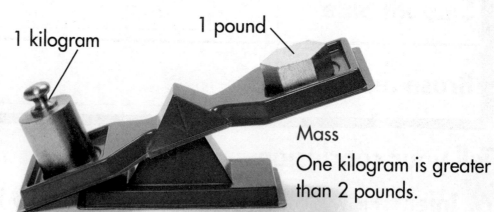

1 kilogram

1 pound

Mass
One kilogram is greater
than 2 pounds.

1 meter

1 foot

Length and Distance
One meter is longer than 3 feet.

Glossary

The glossary uses letters and signs to show how words are pronounced. The mark ′ is placed after a syllable with a primary or heavy accent. The mark ′ is placed after a syllable with a secondary or lighter accent.

To hear these words and definitions, go online to access the digital glossary.

A

aquarium (ə kwär′ ē əm) A water environment in a glass tank or bowl. A pet fish lives in an **aquarium.**

acuario Medio ambiente acuático en un recipiente de cristal. Un pez mascota vive en un **acuario.**

attract (ə trakt′) To pull toward. Magnets **attract** some objects.

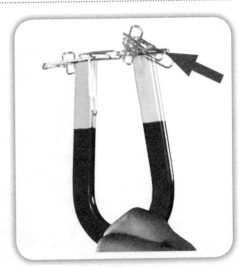

atraer Jalar. Los imanes **atraen** algunos objetos.

data (dā′ tə) Information you collect. You can record **data** about animals.

datos Información que reúnes. Puedes anotar **datos** acerca de los animales.

desert (dez′ ərt) Environment that is very dry. Many plants and animals live in the **desert.**

desierto Medio ambiente que es muy seco. En el **desierto** viven muchas plantas y animales diferentes.

electricity (i lek′ tris′ ə tē) Energy that makes lamps and other things work. The lamp uses **electricity** to work.

electricidad Energía que hace que las lámparas y otros objetos funcionen. La lámpara usa **electricidad** para poder funcionar.

energy (en′ ər jē) Something that can cause change or do work. Moving water has **energy.**

energía Algo que puede causar un cambio o hacer que algo funcione. La corriente de agua tiene **energía.**

environment (en vī′ rən mənt) All
living and nonliving things in one place.
Animals, plants, and rocks are part of an
environment.

medio ambiente Todos los seres vivos
y objetos inertes que hay en un lugar.
Animales, plantas y rocas son parte de un
medio ambiente.

evaporate (i vap′ ə rāt′) To change
from a liquid to a gas. The fire makes the
water in the pot **evaporate.**

evaporar Cambiar de líquido a gas.
El fuego hace que el agua de la olla
se **evapore.**

food chain (füd chān) How energy moves from one living thing to another. A frog eats a grasshopper to get energy. The frog and the grasshopper are part of a **food chain.**

cadena alimenticia Paso de la energía de un ser vivo a otro. Una rana se come un saltamontes para obtener energía. La rana y el saltamontes son parte de la **cadena alimenticia.**

force (fôrs) A push or a pull. The boy uses **force** to move the cart.

fuerza Empujón o jalón. El niño usa **fuerza** para mover el carro.

forest (fôr′ ist) Land that has many trees and other plants. Some bears live in the **forest.**

bosque Medio ambiente que tiene muchos árboles y otras plantas. Algunos osos viven en el **bosque.**

freeze (frēz) To change from a liquid to a solid. We let water **freeze** to make ice cubes.

congelar Cambiar de líquido a sólido. Dejamos **congelar** el agua para hacer cubos de hielo.

G
---

gas (gas) Matter that can change size and shape. The beach toys were full of **gas.**

gas Materia que puede cambiar de tamaño y forma. Los juguetes de playa estaban llenos de **gas.**

H
---

heat (hēt) Moves from warmer places to cooler places. The **heat** from the campfire cooks the food.

calor (o **energía térmica**) Se mueve de lugares más cálidos a lugares más fríos. El **calor** de la hoguera calienta la comida.

humus (hyü′ məs) Small bits of dead plants and animals in soil. Grandmother adds **humus** to the soil to help her plants grow.

humus Restos de plantas y animales muertos en el suelo. Mi abuela le añade **humus** al suelo para ayudar a sus plantas a crecer.

I

inquiry (in kwī′ rē) Looking for answers. You can use **inquiry** to learn about kinds of plants.

indagación Buscar respuestas. Puedes hacer una **indagación** para aprender sobre los tipos de plantas.

investigate (in ves′ tə gāt) To look for answers to questions. Scientists **investigate** to learn about plants.

investigar Buscar respuestas a las preguntas. Los científicos **investigan** para saber más sobre las plantas.

leaf (lēf) The part of a plant that makes food. A **leaf** fell from the rose bush.

hoja La parte de la planta que produce el alimento. Una **hoja** cayó del rosal de mi jardín.

life cycle (līf sī′ kəl) The way a living thing grows and changes. The **life cycle** of a frog includes an egg, a tadpole, a young frog, and an adult frog.

ciclo de vida Manera en que un ser vivo crece y cambia. El **ciclo de vida** de la rana está formado por: huevo, renacuajo, rana joven y rana adulta.

liquid (lik′ wid) Matter that takes the shape of its container. My mother poured the **liquid** into the glasses.

líquido Materia que toma la forma del recipiente que la contiene. Mi mamá puso el **líquido** en los vasos.

living (liv′ ing) Things that can grow and change. The tiger is a **living** thing.

vivo Seres que pueden crecer y cambiar. El tigre es un ser **vivo.**

location (lō kā′ shən) The place where something is. The **location** of the butterfly is near the flower.

ubicación Lugar donde está algo. La **ubicación** de la mariposa está cerca de la flor.

— **M** —

magnet (mag′ nit) An object that attracts some metals. I picked up the paper clips with the **magnet.**

imán Objeto que atrae algunos metales. Recogí los clips con el **imán.**

mass (mas) The amount of matter in an object. The table has **mass.**

masa Cantidad de materia de un objeto. La mesa tiene **masa.**

matter (mat′ ər) Anything that takes up space. Everything around you is made of **matter.**

materia Cualquier cosa que ocupa espacio. Todo lo que hay a nuestro alrededor está hecho de **materia.**

measure (mezh′ ər) To use a tool to find the size or amount of something. You can use a ruler to **measure** how long something is.

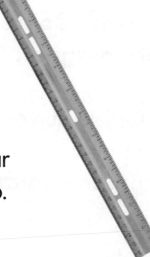

medir Usar un instrumento para saber el tamaño o la cantidad de algo. Puedes usar una regla para **medir** el largo de un objeto.

melt (melt) To change from a solid to a liquid. The ice began to **melt** in the sun.

derretir Cambiar de sólido a líquido. El hielo empezó a **derretirse** bajo el Sol.

natural resource (nach′ ər əl ri sôrs′) A useful material found in nature. Water is a **natural resource.**

recurso natural Material útil que se encuentra en la naturaleza. El agua es un **recurso natural.**

need (nēd) Something a living thing must have to live. Plants grow when their **needs** are met.

necesidad Algo que un ser vivo necesita para vivir. Las plantas crecen cuando se satisfacen sus **necesidades.**

nonliving (non liv′ ing) Things that do not grow and change on their own. Toys are **nonliving** things.

inerte Cosas que no crecen y que no cambian por sí mismas. Los juguetes son objetos **inertes.**

nutrients (nü′ trē ənts) Materials that living things need. Plants need **nutrients** to change and grow.

nutrientes Sustancias que los seres vivos necesitan. Las plantas necesitan **nutrientes** para cambiar y crecer.

observe (əb zėrv′) When you use your senses. You can **observe** sounds that an animal makes.

observar Cuando usas tus sentidos. Puedes **observar** los sonidos que hace un animal.

ocean (ō′ shən) Environment that is a large body of salty water. Some fish live in an **ocean** environment.

océano Medio ambiente que es una gran masa de agua salada. El medio ambiente donde viven algunos peces es el **océano.**

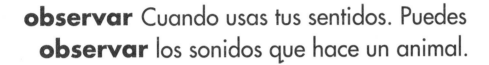

parent (pâr′ ənt) A living thing that has young. The kitten needs its parent to take care of it.

padres Seres vivos que tienen crías. El gatito necesita que sus **padres** lo cuiden.

prairie (prâr′ ē) Environment that is covered with grasses. Some gophers live on **prairies.**

pradera Medio ambiente cubierto de pasto. Algunas tuzas viven en las **praderas.**

predator (pred′ ə tər) An animal that catches and eats another animal. A fox is a fierce **predator.**

predador Animal que caza y se alimenta de otro animal. Un zorro es un **predador** feroz.

prey (prā) An animal that is caught and eaten. Rabbits are **prey.**

presa Animal que es cazado y comido. Los conejos pueden ser una **presa.**

record (ri kôrd′) When scientists write or draw what they learn. It is important to **record** information during experiments.

Favorite Animals				
cat				
dog				
bird				

anotar Cuando los científicos escriben o dibujan lo que descubren. Es importante **anotar** la información durante un experimento.

recycle (rē sī′ kəl) Make used materials into new materials. You can **recycle** milk jugs.

reciclar Convertir materiales usados en materiales nuevos. Se pueden **reciclar** las jarras de leche.

reduce (ri düs´) Use less. You can **reduce** how much electricity you use.

reducir Usar menos. Se puede **reducir** la cantidad de electricidad que usamos.

repel (ri pel´) To push away. The north poles of two magnets placed together will **repel** each other.

repeler Apartar. Los polos norte de dos imanes se **repelen** si se los acerca.

reuse (rē yüz´) Use again. You can **reuse** a metal can.

reutilizar Volver a usar. Puedes **reutilizar** los botes de metal.

root (rüt) The part of a plant that takes in water. We covered the **roots** of the rose plant with soil.

raíz La parte de la planta que toma el agua. Cubrimos las **raíces** del rosal con tierra.

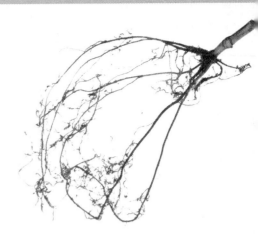

rotation (rō tā′ shən) One spin around. Earth makes one **rotation** each day.

rotación Dar una vuelta sobre sí mismo. La Tierra hace una **rotación** cada día.

safety (sāf′ tē) Staying out of danger. The girl washes her hands to stay **safe.**

seguridad Estar fuera de peligro. La niña se lava las manos para mantenerse **segura.**

season (sē′ zn) A time of year. Spring is my favorite **season.**

estación Período del año. La primavera es mi **estación** favorita.

shadow (shad′ ō) Dark shape made when something blocks light. The tree makes a **shadow** on the ground.

sombra Forma oscura que se forma cuando algo bloquea la luz. El árbol forma una **sombra** en el suelo.

shelter (shel′ tər) A safe place. The beaver uses sticks and mud for **shelter.**

refugio Lugar seguro. El castor usa palitos y lodo para su **refugio.**

soil (soil) The top layer of Earth. You can find rocks in **soil.**

suelo La capa superior de la Tierra. Puedes hallar rocas en el **suelo.**

solid (sol′ id) Matter that has its own shape and size. Each toy in the box is a **solid.**

sólido Materia que tiene forma y tamaño propios. Todos los juguetes de la caja son **sólidos.**

speed (spēd) How quickly or slowly an object moves. The racecar moved at a very fast **speed.**

rapidez Qué tan rápido o tan lento se mueve algo. El carro de carreras se mueve con mucha **rapidez.**

stem (stem) The part of a plant that takes water from the roots to the leaves. The rose's **stem** has sharp thorns.

tallo La parte de una planta que conduce el agua de las raíces a las hojas. El **tallo** del rosal tiene espinas filosas.

T

tadpole (tad′ pōl′) A very young frog. A **tadpole** hatched from the egg.

renacuajo Rana muy joven. El **renacuajo** salió del huevo.

temperature (tem′ per ə chər) How hot or cold something is. It was hot today, and the **temperature** outside was very high.

temperatura Cuán caliente o frío está algo. Hoy la **temperatura** al aire libre estuvo muy alta.

tool (tül) Something that makes work easier. A hand lens is a **tool** that helps you see things.

instrumento Algo que hace más fácil el trabajo. Una lupa es un **instrumento** que te ayuda a ver cosas.

vibrate (vī′ brāt) To move back and forth very fast. Sound happens when objects **vibrate.**

vibrar Mover hacia adelante y hacia atrás muy rápidamente. El sonido se produce cuando los objetos **vibran.**

water vapor (wȯ′ tər vā′ pər) Water that is a gas. When liquid water evaporates, it changes to a gas called **water vapor.**

vapor de agua Agua que es gas. Cuando se evapora el agua líquida, se convierte en un gas llamado **vapor de agua.**

weather (weᴛʜ′ ər) What it is like outside. I like to drink hot chocolate when the **weather** outside is cold.

estado del tiempo Cómo está afuera. Me gusta tomar chocolate caliente cuando el **estado del tiempo** es frío.

weight (wāt) How heavy an object is. You can measure the **weight** of an object.

peso Cuán pesado es un objeto. Puedes medir el **peso** de un objeto.

wetland (wet′ land′) Environment that is covered with water. Tanya saw a blue heron when she visited the **wetland** near her home.

humedal Medio ambiente cubierto de agua. Tanya vio una garza ceniza cuando fue al **humedal** que queda cerca de su casa.

Index

Page numbers for pictures, charts, graphs, maps, and their associated text are printed in *italic type*.

Credits

Photographs

Every effort has been made to secure permission and provide appropriate credit for photographic material. The publisher deeply regrets any omission and pledges to correct errors called to its attention in subsequent editions.

Unless otherwise acknowledged, all photographs are the property of Pearson Education, Inc.

COVER: Howard Noel/Shutterstock

Title l Creatix/Fotolia; Title c jojje11/Fotolia; TitleBkgrd Larry Landolfi/Science Source/Photo Researchers, Inc.; Title plant Image Studio/Getty Images; iv HG Photography/Fotolia; v Radius Images/Alamy; vii Jamesbenet /iStockphoto; viii Q-Images/Alamy; ix Jim Parkin/Shutterstock; x Bernd Zoller/Imagebroker/Alamy; xi Corey Hochachka/Vibe Images/Alamy; xvii br iStockphoto; xix b Bloomau/Fotolia; 000 Banner TX flag Brandon Seidel/Fotolia; 000Bkgd Masterfile; 002 DK Images; 005 Corbis/Jupiter Images; 008 Zefa/SuperStock; 008Bkgd REB Images/Blend Images/Getty Images; 009B Morgan Lane Photography/Alamy; 009T Asia Images Group Pte Ltd/Alamy; 010Bkgd Zastolskiy Victor/Shutterstock; 011 Chris Ryan/Alamy; 012 Angela M. Wyro/National Natural Toxins Research Center; 012Bkgd Shackleford Photography/Shutterstock; 012C Shmel/Shutterstock; 016Bkgd Robyn Mackenzie/Shutterstock; 017 Jupiterimages/Getty Images/Thinkstock; 018 Carlos Davila/Photographer's Choice RF/Getty Images; 020Bkgd Don Klumpp/Alamy; 022 James Godman/Alamy; 023T Glow Wellness/SuperStock; 024R Lucato/Fotolia; 025CR Devulderj/Fotolia; 026BR Kruwt/Fotolia; 026TL Dmitry Rukhlenko/Fotolia; 026TR Scrapimg/Fotolia; 027BL Dave King/DK Images; 027BR Dave King/DK Images; 027T Terex/Fotolia; 028 Indeed/Getty Images; 032Bkgd Davis Barber/PhotoEdit; 033inset Images of Africa Photobank/Alamy; 035T Getty Images/Jupiterimages; 036Bkgd Design Pics/SuperStock; 038Bkgd Martin Ruegner/StockImage/Getty Images; 040T BananaStock/Jupiter Images; 041B Comstock/Jupiter Images; 041T BananaStock/Jupiter Images; 044 Devin Boldt-NASA-JSC; 045BL Davis Barber/PhotoEdit; 045CL Indeed/Getty Images; 045CR Jupiterimages/Getty Images/Thinkstock; 045TR Zefa/SuperStock; 047T Radius Images/Alamy; 049B Herry Choi/TongRo Images/Alamy; 049TL JupiterImages; 049TR JupiterImages; 051BL Davis Barber/PhotoEdit; 051BR Radius Images/Alamy; 051TC Jupiterimages/Getty Images/Thinkstock; 051TL Zefa/SuperStock; 058 Joseph Calev/shutterstock; 060 VanHart/Shutterstock; 062 Robert Mayne USA/Alamy; 066Bkgd Scruggelgreen/Fotolia; 067BL Matthew Cole/Shutterstock; 074Bkgd Amar and Isabelle Guillen/Guillen Photography/Alamy; 074L Rick Sargeant/Fotolia; 075 Amar and Isabelle Guillen/Guillen Photography/Alamy; 079B Andy Dean/Fotolia; 079C Titan/Fotolia; 079T ImageDJ/Alamy; 084 WorldFoto/Alamy; 085TR Masterfile Royalty-Free; 089BC Heros1973/Fotolia; 089BL Oleg Ivanov/Fotolia; 089BR Mbongo/Fotolia; 090 Anetlanda/Fotolia; 094 foodfolio/Alamy; 097 Mark Owen/Blackout Concepts/Alamy; 102B ArchMan/Shutterstock; 102T Photos to Go/Photolibrary; 103T Bethany Dawn/DK Images; 104 Dave King/D K Images; 104 Dave King/DK images; 104Bkgd Randall Stevens/Shutterstock;

106 Goodshoot/Getty Images/Jupiterimages; 108Bkgd Masterfile Royalty Free; 108Bkgd Masterfile; 109BR Roman Sigaev/Fotolia; 109TR Preto perola/Fotolia; 112Bkgd Jamesbenet/Istockphoto; 113C Thinkstock Images/Comstock/Getty Images/Jupiterimages; 113L Comstock/Jupiterimages; 114B Topora/Shutterstock; 114T Numb/Alamy; 115 Jupiterimages; 115Bkgd Craig Wactor/Fotolia; 116 Chris Jones; 120 Erik Isakson/Rubberball/Getty Images; 121B Jozsef Szasz-Fabian/Shutterstock; 121Bkgd Leonid Shcheglov/Shutterstock; 121C Dmitriy Bryndin/Shutterstock; 121T WojciechBeczynski/Shutterstock; 122B Jacek Chabraszewski/shutterstock; 122Bkgd Masterfile; 122T Comstock Images/Jupiterimages; 123Bkgd Thomas M Perkins/shutterstock; 123R Comstock/Jupiter images; 124CR Tim Ridley/DK Images; 124BR Anetlanda/Fotolia; 124CR Andy Crawford/DK Images; 126 Jim Parkin/Fotolia; 127CL Erik Isakson/Rubberball/Getty Images; 131B Dmitriy Bryndin/Shutterstock; 131TC Creatas Images/Jupiterimages; 131TC Creatas Images/Jupiterimages; 131TC Creatas Images/Jupiterimages; 131TR Jamesbenet /Istockphoto; 134 Maisie Paterson/Stone/Getty Images; 137 Exactostock/SuperStock; 138Bkgd Dave Welling/Jaynes Gallery/Danita Delimont/Alamy; 140Bkgd Wendy Connett / Alamy; 141 Fuse/Jupiterimages; 142B Vladimir Volkov/Fotolia; 142C K3/Ikon Images/Alamy; 142T John Cordes/Icon SMI 506/Newscom; 144Bkgd Q-Images/Alamy; 145 Juergen Lotz/Ap Images; 148Bkgd Kirk Geisler/Shutterstock.com; 149B Lasse Kristensen/Fotolia; 149C Comstock/Jupiterimages; 150 Myrleen Pearson/PhotoEdit; 152Bkgd Chad Palmer/Shutterstock; 159B Igor Kovalchuk/Fotolia; 161Bkgd Wang Song/Shutterstock; 164B Vadim/Fotolia; 164BR Ruta Saulyte/Fotolia; 167 Vladimir Volkov/Fotolia; 167BM Yellowj/Fotolia; 167TR Vladimir Volkov/Fotolia; 167TR Vladimir Volkov/Fotolia; 169 Jupiter Images; 171B RubberBall/SuperStock; 171TC Comstock/Jupiterimages; 171TL Vladimir Volkov/Fotolia; 176 George H.H. Huey/Alamy; 181T Rob Byron/Shutterstock; 184Bkgd Photos To Go; 186B Jupiter Images; 186Bkgd Derrick Neill/Fotolia; 186C Hemera Technologies/Jupiter Images; 188 Kevin Eaves/Shutterstock; 188M Bob Daemmrich/Alamy; 188R Jupiterimages/Thinkstock; 190 Terry Reimink/Fotolia; 192 Iwona Grodzka/Shutterstock; 194Bkgd Randy Green/Alamy; 195 CLM/Shutterstock; 196C DK Images; 197 BWAC Images/Alamy; 198B Witold Skrypczak/Alamy; 198T Clint Farlinger/Alamy; 199Bkgd Andy Crawford/DK images; 199T Photolibrary; 200BL Pix/Alamy; 200BR Tracy Collins/Flickr Open/Getty Images; 200T Terry Vine/The Image Bank/Getty Images; 201B Jeannie Burleson/Alamy; 201C Don Klumpp/Alamy; 201T Lyroky/Alamy; 202Bkgd John Elk III/Alamy; 204Bkgd Hestamm/Fotolia; 205 James Warwick/The Image Bank/Gettyimages; 206 Sue Ashe/Shutterstock; 207L Coto Elizondo/Gettyimages; 207R Allan Shoemake/Gettyimages; 208B Feng Yu/Alamy; 208T Robert Dant/Alamy; 212Bkgd Chris Howes/Wild Places Photography/Alamy; 213L William H. Edwards/Photodisc/Getty Images; 213R Lorie Leigh Lawrence/Alamy; 214L Tristan3D / Alamy; 215R Tristan3D / Alamy; 216 Vetrova/Shutterstock; 220 Jim Cummins/Taxi/Getty Images; 226Bkgd Lakov Kalinin/Fotolia; 227B Siede Preis/Photodisc/Getty Images; 227T Annie Reynolds/Photodisc/Getty Images; 228B Blend Images/Alamy;

Take Note

This space is yours. Draw pictures and write words.

This is your book. You can write in it.

This is your book. You can write in it.

This is your book. You can write in it.

This is your book. You can write in it.

This is your book. You can write in it.

This is your book. You can write in it.